EGY...

QUEST

by
Herbie Brennan

Kingfisher

Kingfisher
An Imprint of Larousse plc
Elsey House
24-30 Great Titchfield Street
London
W1P 7AD

10 9 8 7 6 5 4 3 2 1

A CIP catalogue record for this book is available from the British
Library.

ISBN 0 7534 0090 1

Herbie Brennan has asserted his moral right to be identified as the
author of the work in accordance with the Copyright, Designs and
Patents Act, 1988.

Designed and typeset by Val Carless
Printed in the United Kingdom
by Cox & Wyman Ltd, Reading, Berkshire.

It's the year 350 B.C. and you've just realised
you never should have gone on the school trip
to the British Museum.

And certainly you never should have made that
bet with Spider Simpson.

Because Spider challenged you to spend the
night in a sarcophagus in the Egyptian Rooms.

And now somehow you're back in Ancient Egypt
in the time of the wizard king,
Pharaoh Nectanebo II.

But that's not the worst of it.

Because the Pharaoh wants your help in
fighting off the Persian invaders. And that
means risking your life in a race against time.

In this incredible new solo gamebook you will
adventure through the most fascinating
culture humanity has ever known.

A culture where the king is god.

Where magic is a fact of life.

And where you'll be stuck forever if you don't
find the lost treasure of the pyramids!

IMPORTANT: READ THIS FIRST!

You can't just read this book – you have to live it.

To do that, you'll need pen and paper to keep a record of any weapons, magic potions, etc, and your number of Life Points. You'll also need a couple of dice and to learn the game play system.

Of course, you may have played another of the books in this series. In which case you'll know exactly what to do.

But if this is your first book, turn now to the section headed GAME PLAY SYSTEM at the back.

Otherwise, you can turn to the next page and get straight on with your adventure ...

You look around. On your left, in a niche, is a life-size statue of Sekhmet, the lion-headed goddess of war. Ahead is a five metre high stela, covered in neatly carved hieroglyphs. And beside you is the massive granite sarcophagus of Pharaoh Nectanebo II, covered not only in hieroglyphs, but in Japanese tourists.

The clickety-click-click of their cameras echoes in your ears like an attack of the deathwatch beetle, and you wonder if this gallery will ever empty, even for the moment you need.

Nonchalantly you stroll around the various exhibits. Here is a little statue of Bastet, the cat goddess, looking cute and proud. There is a representation of the falcon sky god Horus. Here Khepri, the scarab beetle, there Khonsu, the moon god of Thebes, beside a display stand of booklets marked *A BRIEF HISTORY OF ANCIENT EGYPT. PLEASE TAKE ONE.* Never one to miss a freebie, you drop a copy into your pocket.

You walk a little further. A sign to one side announces:

ROSETTA STONE THIS WAY ➡

Beyond it, another sign announces:

⬅ ANUBIS RELIEF THAT WAY

If you want to see the Rosetta Stone, whatever that is, go to 99. But if you're curious to find out why Anubis was so relieved, you should turn to 67.

"You win," you tell him. "I'll have this hideous thing."

"Good choice!" he beams. "That's a sacred scarab – brings you a whole heap of good luck. As we haven't invented money here in Egypt yet, you have to pay me by doing a little service instead."

This is turning into a real nightmare. You can tell him to keep his stupid scarab and stalk off to 103 to select another destination. But if you still want to buy it, you'll find out about his 'little service' at 150.

"Look," you say, "I'm flattered, of course, and I really would like to help, but I have to be getting back, you know – school work and that, homework, parents, disco on Saturday. Anywhere that suits you. Just drop me off at the British Museum if it's handy." You smile brightly.

"Would it change your mind if I threatened to kill you?" Nectanebo asks.

If you'd prefer Nectanebo to kill you, just say so now and he can send you to 13 with a wave of his magical left hand. But since it's everybody's privilege to change their mind, you'll still be more than welcome at 15.

4

You begin to scrabble around in the sand.

A process that involves throwing two dice. Score ...

1. and you've begun to hallucinate.
2. and you find nothing, although you can come back again – after returning to 103 and exploring another destination.
3. and you find nothing, but are allowed another dice roll.
4. and you find a healing potion that will restore a double dice roll of Life Points. You can only return to search this section again after you've used the healing potion.
5. and you find a healing potion that will restore a double dice roll of Life Points. You can search this section again immediately by making another dice throw.
6. and you find a short supernatural rod of polished amethyst which will cause one enemy to fall asleep. Roll one die to find out how many times you can use the rod. You can only search this section again after using the rod at least once.
7. and you find a priestly healing wand which will instantly restore you to your maximum Life Points at any time. It only has one charge, so save it for an emergency. You may search this section again at once if you wish.
8. and you find an absolutely vicious +12 club. Unfortunately

it's so heavy you can only use it every second combat round. You can only return to search this section again after you've used the club at least once.

9. and you find the papyrus map shown at 75.

10. and you're stung by a scorpion for the loss of a double dice roll of Life Points. If this kills you, go to 13. If it doesn't, the poison will cause the loss of a single die roll of Life Points in each of the next five sections you visit. You can search this section again immediately, but if you're stung by any more scorpions, the effect is cumulative.

11. and you find several papyrus pages from a book by someone called Herodotus at 125. Meanwhile, you can search this section again at once if you wish.

12. and you find what seems to be a secret trapdoor, but actually isn't. Despite the disappointment, you can search this section again immediately if you wish.

At any time you can go to 103 to select another destination.

<5>

"Not interested," you say firmly.

"It's a very good map. Very genuine. There are two secret entrances. It shows them both."

"I'm sorry," you say, moving to walk away.

He grabs you by the arm. "One's at ground level, the other's directly above it. Quarter twist to open the secret doors. Now how would I know that if the map wasn't genuine."

You turn to look him in the eye.

"Read my lips," you say. "I do ... not ... want ... your ... map!"

"Take that then," he says, bopping you on the nose and running nimbly away.

That blow to the nose was a lot more painful than it looked. In fact it's removed no fewer than 5 of your Life Points. If this kills you, go to 13. If you've survived, you might think about what the little man said at 80.

"There's absolutely no way I'm about to go off with a bunch of bald old coots!" you yell rudely, hurling yourself upon them.

Which is where things get complicated. First off, each of these three closely shaven priests sports 50 Life Points and carries a +5 dagger, but for every one of them you manage to kill, another two will pile in from the courtyard outside. There is absolutely no way you can win the fight.

The priests will do their best to knock you unconscious by bringing your Life Points below five. If they manage, they'll revive you and drag you off to 136. If, they accidentally bring your Life Points down to zero in the process, go to 13.

As you begin to move downwards, you start to realise how steep this passage really is. And how slippery. In fact it's so slippery you can hardly keep on your feet.

Throw one die. Score 1, 2 or 3 and you lose your footing completely so you bash your skull on the floor with such violence that all your brains ooze out in a filthy mess, thus making life just a little bit easier for the embalmers who are patiently waiting for you at 13. Score 4, 5 or 6 and you keep on your feet sufficiently to face more passage perils at 23.

This is unbelievable. The structure towering above you is like a mountain – by far the biggest of the three main pyramids on this site. Now you're close up, you can estimate its base at seven New York city blocks! The glistening whiteness you could see from a distance comes from the fact that the entire pyramid has been covered in a layer of polished limestone.

You reach for your **Brief History of Ancient Egypt.** Leafing through, you find the part on the Great Pyramid of Cheops. There's a picture, and while the limestone casing has gone, it's obviously the same structure as the one you're looking at now.

What you read is almost as awesome as the pyramid itself. It rises in 201 stepped tiers to its golden pyramidion cap (that's gone in the picture as well!). It has more stone in it than all the churches, chapels and cathedrals built in England from the time of Christ to the day of your birth. It was built by some old Pharaoh called Cheops, but that was only the Greek version of his name. His actual name in Egyptian was Khufu.
After a moment you find what you've been looking for.

Sometime after his ascension to the throne of Egypt in A.D. 813, Caliph Mamum was told the Great Pyramid had a secret chamber which contained accurate maps of the world, arms that would not rust, glass that would bend but not break, and a vast treasure.

Excited by this information, he put together in A.D. 820 a force of engineers, architects, stone masons and builders and instructed them to find the lost entrance to the pyramid.

For days the Caliph's men vainly searched the sloping sides of the immense structure until their patience failed and they decided to break in ...

If they had only known it, the secret doorway for which they were searching actually lay just a little above the spot where they broke in, on the face of the pyramid that lies to the ...

You turn the page quickly to find out where the secret entrance to the pyramid is located.

*... until the time of Cleopatra
who had herself delivered to
Julius Caesar in a carpet.*

Some little idiot has torn a page out of the *Brief History of Ancient Egypt,* probably to read the naughty bits about Cleopatra and Caesar! You stand fuming with rage.

But when the smoke stops rising from your ears, you still have to find your way in to the pyramid. If you want to search the eastern face of the pyramid for the secret entrance, turn to 25. You can search the south face at 41, the west face at 57 and the north face at 68. Or you can turn back to your map at 103 and select another destination.

9

As you approach the now empty sarcophagus, you can see a hieroglyphic inscription so faded that it's clear it will have vanished altogether in a few years. But your eagle eye discerns:

To activate the time gate, climb into the sarcophagus, then say the correct two of the following names aloud. But beware – the wrong two names will lead to death.

Underneath the message are the following names:

Osiris, Horus, Khufu, Sekhmet and Khefra

You climb into the sarcophagus and prepare to intone two names.

But which two?! Khufu and Khefra send you to 19; Horus and Khufu to 38; Osiris and Sekhmet to 66; Horus and Osiris to 81; Osiris and Khufu to 105; Horus and Sekhmet to 110; Khefra and Horus to 121; Khufu and Sekhmet to 137; Osiris and Khefra to 143; Sekhmet and Khefra to 159.

10

You should have known. Could 13, Funeral Street, be anything but an undertaker's address? Or, more accurately, an undertaker's and embalmer's? The character who takes the package says dolefully:

"We were waiting for this. It's for the dear departed. We're mummifying him right now. Want to watch? It's interesting, but sort of gruesome."

If you want to watch, go to 52. But if you'd rather wave a fond farewell to Funeral Street, you can do that at 59.

There is a sound like a thunderclap. Your eyes are blinded by a great white light. The world begins to whirl around you as your soul is swept from your body and propelled through a narrow shaft upwards and out of the great stone structure.

You hurtle skywards at escape velocity, up, up, up beyond the very atmosphere and yet your speed does not diminish. Glancing down you realise you can see the curvature of the Earth, and in a moment you see your home planet as a vast blue sphere.

And still your journey does not end, for you streak out of the solar system heading for deep space. Your mind dissolves in ecstasy as you travel on, and on, and on, and on. Until ...

You halt. You expand. You combust. You shine. The vast nuclear furnaces within your frame roar and rumble with the fires of heaven, as you howl in purest joy.

You might like to know you've gone the way of the old Egyptian Pharaohs who believed that when they died, their souls became one with the great transpolar stars. However, it means all you can do now is shine for 20,000,000 years or so until you become a Red Giant or White Dwarf or Black Hole – at which point you can crawl back gratefully to 13.

Cautiously you approach the altar. The great statue of Osiris seems to stare down on you, but whether with a smile or frown is difficult to say in the flickering light.

You lick your lips nervously, then reach for the jewelled flail on the altar. As you touch it, there is a savage growling noise behind you.

You swing round, expecting an attack from a wild beast, but the growling is caused by the stone slab moving from the doorway. Snatching Osiris' flail from the altar, you run for the exit.

As you enter the colonnaded hall beyond, the flail twitches in your hand to point like a divining rod at one of the exits. You find yourself guided through a maze of passages until you arrive at two marvellously preserved wooden doors, one faced in gold, the other in silver. This time the flail lies inert in your hand.

It's make-your-mind-up time again. It's not much help, but the silver door leads to 138 while the golden door opens onto 50.

Well, that's it. You're dead, deceased, no longer living. You've turned your toes up, snuffed it. You are now a late adventurer.

The good news is there's a lot of life after death in this book. Climb out of your mummy case, re-roll your Life Points, not forgetting to add on any Permanent Points you've notched up due to experience, and start, intrepidly, again.

Better luck next time.

These holes look as if they once carried wooden cross-pieces, so there *was* a time when the ascending passage moved so steeply that it blocked off the entrance to the horizontal passage: it was once completely secret. You look upwards and notice the gloomy entrance to yet another passageway high above.

Will you negotiate the shaft at 76, explore the formerly secret horizontal passage at 129, take the descending passage to return to your map at 103, or risk a climb up to the dark entrance above the horizontal passage at 26?

Nectanebo stretches and pokes his lion playfully with his toe.

"Since I became able to see the future, I've known for some time these wretched Persians might get the better of me. But the future can always be changed. All I need's a little help. Somewhere in the pyramids of Giza are wonderful weapons and mysterious artefacts from Egypt's ancient past. That treasure can make Egypt invincible. You must find it. When you do, send word by means of this homing pigeon. I chose you because, being from the future, you'll know where to find the various secret passageways we have not yet discovered."

You open your mouth to tell him you certainly don't, when he adds, "Besides, you have a special incentive."

"What's that?" you ask suspiciously.

Nectanebo gives you a brilliant smile. "I can bring people here but I can't send them back. The only way for you to get home is by means of a special time gate you'll find with the treasure."

"How do I get to the Giza complex?" you sigh, stowing the pigeon (and some corn) away in a convenient pocket.

"Pronounce this spell aloud and you'll know exactly what to do."

Read the hieroglyphic words aloud and do what they tell you. (If you're having trouble translating, cheat with a peek at 99!)

"You win," you tell him. "I'll have this hideous thing."

"Good choice!" he beams. "That's a sacred Eye of Horus."

"How much is it?"

"You know we haven't invented money here in Egypt yet, so you have to do me a little service instead."

This is turning into a real nightmare. You can tell him to keep his stupid Eye of Horus and stalk off to 103 to select another destination. But if you still want to buy it, you'll find out about his 'little service' at 150.

You run like the wind and quickly out-distance your pursuers. Only when you are hidden in a deserted alley do you notice your surroundings. You are in a sun-drenched city, the like of which you have never seen before – or even imagined.

Although you are now certain you have somehow managed to return to Ancient Egypt, to a time before the development of technology, the city is little short of amazing! The roads and streets are paved, the buildings set out in a grid that would do justice to New York. The mud brick houses are sturdily made and everything is brightly decorated in strong, primary colours.

But what impresses you most is the monumental statuary, towering obelisks and massive stone temples. The scale is nothing short of awesome.

As you emerge from the alley, you find yourself in a small market place which not only offers a bewildering array of fruits and vegetables, but also allows you to watch a variety of craftsmen at work. Two carpenters use a bow-drill to make a highly ornamental bed ... a young man is pounding cross-latticed reeds with a mallet to make papyrus paper ... a hawk-nosed jeweller squats beside a small table, patiently rolling pieces of rose quartz beneath a special board to polish them.

The jeweller looks up as you walk past. "Want a magic ring?" he asks. "I need to deliver a bead collar, and I'm offering a magic ring to anybody who'll do the job. Are you interested?"

If you want a magic ring, turn to 35. If you've got better things to do, tell old beak-nose to get lost at 91.

The passageway climbs steeply upwards until it is suddenly blocked by a stone slab.

By now you've developed a strong suspicion that stone slabs blocking passages seldom mark the end of the road, but rather some stupid (and often dangerous) puzzle, so you examine the surface of the slab. Sure enough, there is a message engraved on it, in a weird mix of hieroglyphs and ancient runes:

Let's hope you can make some sense of this. But if not, you can always go back the way you came and take the downward sloping passage at 7, or leave the pyramid completely and return to 103 where you can select another destination.

No sooner have the names passed your lips than your head explodes.

Clean up the mess and go to 13.

Although half-buried in the sand, you recognise the enormous figure at once. The lion body and the human head are unmistakable. You have reached the Great Sphinx, a gigantic sculpture built, according to your *Brief History of Ancient Egypt,* at the same time as the pyramids.

Or maybe not. The guide mentions a recent controversy about weathering patterns on the statue which suggest it might have been erected earlier – possibly very much earlier.

The head of the sphinx is supposed to be a portrait of King Khefra – the one the Greeks called Kephren. You are still staring up at the huge statue when a little old Egyptian woman shuffles by. "They call it the Father of Terror, you know," she tells you.

"I can see why it would frighten people."

"No you can't," says the old lady sharply. "You think it gets that name because it's half a lion and very big. But it doesn't. It's called Father of Terror because of what it guards."

Intrigued, you ask, "What does it guard?"

"Secret chambers," says the old woman promptly. "Very dangerous indeed. They say the entrance is somewhere between the paws, but with all this sand you'd have to do a lot of digging before you'd find it now." She tosses her head and shuffles off.

If you want to try your hand at searching, you can do so at 4. As against that, you may want to save yourself a lot of time by returning to 103 and picking another destination.

⟨21⟩

The passageway you have entered slopes steeply downwards. You follow it cautiously until it levels off in a small ante-chamber. You glance around, but there is nothing to interest you.

From the ante-chamber a short stretch of corridor takes you to a much larger chamber cut into the bedrock, well below the mass of the pyramid itself. You note the outlines of what seems to be a trapdoor dead in the centre of the floor. Beyond it, you can see an ascending passageway leading out of the chamber.

You can try opening the trapdoor at 33 or leave this chamber by the ascending passage at 46.

⟨22⟩

"That's a double-headed coin!" you shout.

"Isn't!" screams the little man.

"Is!" you yell.   "Isn't!"   "Is!!"

And so it goes on like a political discussion until you finally come to blows.

You now learn the little man has an almost unbelievable 100 Life Points and carries a crude firearm imported from China. This can only be used once, but hits with a massive 30 points, after which the man will attack with a Samurai sword which hits with +15. If you survive you can collect up the ankh, the scarab and both Bastet statues and select another destination from your map at 103. If not, limp along to 13.

You continue to move down the passage until, to your horror, you find there is an opening in the floor. There's a good chance you can jump it, but as against that, the passage still slopes steeply and is still slippery. So even if you don't fall in, you may break your neck. You begin to wonder if you should be going on this way at all.

You can retrace your steps and take the upward sloping passage at 18, or go out to 103 and pick another destination. If you decide to jump the opening in the floor, it's Absolutely Anything Roll time again. Should the attempt kill you, turn to 13. If you succeed you can continue down the passage at 34. If you fail, you've gone straight into the floor opening at 51.

You pick up one of the little oil lamps for light and make your way to the passageway. The floor slopes upwards so that after a time you find yourself breathing heavily. You catch your breath by pausing to look at an intriguing wall painting showing two Egyptian sailors. You continue to climb until the passage ends abruptly in a blank wall. There's no way out!!

You can scream and beat your head violently against this blank wall at 96. Or, if that strikes you as a waste of time, you can trundle back down to explore the ante-chamber at 48 or climb into the sarcophagus with your mummy at 63.

You assume that if there is an entrance anywhere, it's likely to be some distance above ground, otherwise it would have been found before now. You look at the polished limestone casing of the pyramid and move towards the first tier.

For someone as young, fit and courageous as yourself, climbing the pyramid proves quite possible. But it's slow work, made even slower by the fact you're searching for a hidden entrance.

Eventually, after painstaking examination of every block, you conclude that if the pyramid has an entrance at all, it's not on this face. You climb down, experiencing a mixture of disappointment and determination.

But as you reach the ground again, you're seized by two muscle-bound characters whose dress is Egyptian, but whose features you would swear were definitely Persian.

"Tell us what you've found or we'll cut your throat!" one hisses viciously in your left ear.

These two Persian clowns have each got 20 Life Points and are carrying +5 daggers. If, despite your valiant efforts, they kill you, go to 13. If you kill them take the daggers and search the south face at 41, the west face at 57 or the north face at 68. Or, you can turn back to your map at 103 and select another destination.

You clamber up using the joist-holes as foot-holds and pull yourself into the higher entrance. As you stand upright, you can see you are at the bottom of a narrow gallery some nine metres high, stretching away from you at much the same angle as the ascending passage, deep into the heart of this ancient pyramid.

As you move forward, you discover that the ground beneath your feet is so slippery you can scarcely keep your balance.

Which brings you to an Absolutely Anything Roll. If this kills you it means you've slipped and broken your neck, in which case go to 13. If the roll fails, it means you've slipped and fallen out of the gallery for the loss of 10 Life Points. If this kills you, go to 13, if not go back to 71, having fallen on your feet. If the roll succeeds, make your merry way to 47.

<27>

"Hi-ya, Banzai!" you scream, dropping into a karate stance. But the mummies have not heard of Japan and they keep on coming.

This actually isn't quite as bad as it looks. Two of the mummies are so badly bandaged that they fall apart with a single hit against them. Until then, they take turns in the fight and do normal dice damage against you. The third has 15 Life Points but will rip your head off on a natural throw of 12. But he too scores only dice damage with no plusses. If the mummies get you, go to 13. Should you survive, go to 43.

<28>

Cautiously you shake the Pharaoh's hand. "The Pharaoh has been touched!" scream the ushers in unison. "The Pharaoh has been touched! Death must follow! Death must surely follow!"

"Oh, do be quiet!" Nectanebo tells them. "This young person is magically protected." He leans forward and whispers, "I like to encourage the myth – it keeps the peasants in their place, so please do play along." Then he adds more loudly, "Here, take this. You'll be quite safe if you follow it."

He hands you an amulet inscribed with these hieroglyphs:

$$\varrho \cap \mathbin{\text{I}}$$

As Nectanebo says, you'll be okay if you follow it. So follow it. But if you can't, you will be torn to pieces by Nectanebo's subjects, in which case go to 13.

Out

Well, I did try to warn you. Position yourself where it says
'Start' and see if you can find a route through the maze of
passageways underneath the sphinx. If you're unable to find
your way to 'Out' you will eventually starve to death, which will
help you find your way to 13. If you manage to reach the maze
exit successfully, you can turn with some relief to 45.

20

30

"You win," you tell him. "I'll have this hideous thing."

"Good choice!" he beams. "That's a sacred ankh – the gods gave it to the Pharaoh as a sign of life, so you'll find it makes you feel very lively."

"How much is it?"

"You know we haven't invented money here in Egypt yet, so you have to do me a little service instead."

This is turning into a real nightmare. You can tell him to keep his stupid ankh and stalk off to 103 to select another destination. But if you still want to buy it, you'll find out about his 'little service' at 150.

31

There is a sound like a thunderclap. Your eyes are blinded by a great white light. The world begins to whirl around you as your soul is swept from your body and propelled through a narrow shaft upwards and out of the great stone structure.

You hurtle skywards at escape velocity, up, up, up beyond the very atmosphere and yet your speed does not diminish. Glancing down you realise you can see the curvature of the Earth and in a moment you see your home planet as a vast blue sphere.

And still your journey does not end, for you streak out of the solar system heading for deep space. Your mind dissolves in ecstasy as you travel on, and on, and on, and on ... until ...

You halt. You expand. You combust. You shine. The vast nuclear furnaces within your frame roar and rumble with the fires of heaven as you howl in purest joy.

You might like to know you've gone the way of the old Egyptian Pharaohs who believed that when they died, their souls became one with the great transpolar stars. However, it means all you can do now is shine for 20,000,000 years or so until you become a Red Giant or White Dwarf or Black Hole – at which point you can crawl back gratefully to 13.

Cautiously you move further into the gloom of the inner chamber. Close up, the stone construction looks more like a sarcophagus stood on end than a sentry box. Nervously you unfasten the string. The doors swing open of their own accord – your heart leaps into your throat as you see the tall, imposing figure inside.

You step back with a gasp, then realise the figure is actually a realistically painted, life-size statue of a woman wearing a half-moon shaped head-dress with a sun disc in the horns.

You start to relax and your heart beat returns to normal just in time to race again as three totally hairless men burst into the chamber.

"What do you think you're doing looking at the goddess Isis?" one of them screams at you in a strangely archaic tongue which, somehow, you understand perfectly.

If the woman is a goddess, that makes this a temple. Which means these closely shaven men may well be priests. One of the men glares at you. "Only priests are allowed inside the temples."

"I'm a visiting priest," you lie, looking him straight in the eye.

"Then why haven't you shaved every hair off your head and your body like the rest of us?" he asks you slyly. "I'm afraid I'm going to have to ask you to come with us."

Since you're unlikely to convince him you lost your razor, this is beginning to look like a real hassle. If you want to go quietly, you can do so at 136. But if you feel like making trouble (such as beating these goons to a pulp) you can try your luck at 6.

The trapdoor is a broad stone slab, worn and slightly cracked from age. Indentations remain where a metal ring was once attached, and these are large enough for you to slide your fingers in. You lean over to do so, but as your hand touches the slab, the entire floor crumbles suddenly, plunging you downwards through a narrow shaft into total darkness. You pick yourself up and feel around the walls to discover you are in an empty stone-lined chamber ... with no way out. Desperately you try jumping to reach the shaft through which you fell, but it is too high.

I could describe your increasing panic, the slow wasting away from hunger. But let's just say your only way out is via 13.

The passage continues to slope a little distance longer, then levels out. You reach what seems to be an unfinished chamber deep below the pyramid. The floor has been cut in several rough levels so that its lowest point is about four metres below the ceiling. In the centre of the floor is a square pit, while opposite you is an exit passageway in the south wall.

You can investigate the square pit at 95 or go directly into the exit passage at 107.

You can investigate the square pit at 95 or go directly into the exit passage at 107.

"Yeah, okay, sure," you tell him coolly. "Why not?"

The jeweller takes an ornate collar, wraps it neatly in papyrus and writes something on the outside. He next produces an exquisitely carved ring in the shape of a coiled cobra. "There's your magic ring. You can put it on, but don't rub it until you need it: it only works a dozen times before the magic runs out."

The ring fits perfectly and sends a tingle all through your arm. You suddenly feel you're ten feet tall. "Oh, wow, thanks!" you say, forgetting to be cool.

"I've written the address on the package," the jeweller says. Your heart sinks a little as you try to read what he has written:

To find out more about the ring, turn to 132. Meanwhile you'd better deliver the package – if you can make out the jeweller's writing. If you can't, maybe you'd like to cheat by going to 99.

<36>

You follow the sloping passage until it levels out into a stone lined corridor about the height of a tall man. But no more than a few metres down this corridor you find your way blocked by a massive granite slab inscribed with a tight mass of delicately cut hieroglyphs.

With some difficulty you translate the glyphs, which form an intriguing message:

Oh wanderer, to pass beyond this barrier of stone,
pronounce clearly the Egyptian name of the Pharaoh
associated with the smallest of the three great pyramids.

Must be some sort of magical lock. But which of the three ancient Pharaohs is associated with the smallest pyramid? If you think it's Khufu, turn to 69. If you think it's Khefra, go to 84. If you think it's Menkaura turn to 113.

<37>

Nope, no secret entrance here.

You can examine the south face at 65, the east face at 74 or the west face at 145. Or, if you get bored with the whole thing, you can always go back to 103 and select another destination from your map.

<38>

No sooner have the names passed your lips than your head explodes.

Clean up the mess and go to 13.

<39>

You approach a towering pyramid. Your first impression is that it's higher than the others, but when you get closer you see this is an illusion due to the fact it's been built on higher ground. At 143 metres, the structure is actually a few metres smaller than the Great Pyramid beside it.

You drag out your *Brief History of Ancient Egypt* and discover this pyramid was built by King Khefra (Kephren in Greek). He was the son of King Khufu, and got to be Pharaoh in the 26th Century B.C. His pyramid was almost as big as the Great Pyramid of King Khufu, each side measuring 216 metres.

"Pssst!" pssts a voice in your ear. "Want to buy a map that shows every secret entrance to Khefra's pyramid? You can have it for those shoes you're wearing."

A familiar-looking wizened little man has crept up beside you.

Before you answer, I'd better warn you that if you barter your shoes you'll lose 1 Life Point, due to sore feet, every second section you enter. Doesn't sound much, but it mounts up. If you want to do the deal, take your shoes off at 54. If not, turn to 5.

40

Back in 1927, the British archaeologist Howard Carter was excavating in Egypt's Valley of the Kings when he discovered the tomb of a seventeen-year-old Pharaoh called Tutankhamun with its seals unbroken.

This got him really excited. Most tombs of Egyptian Pharaohs had been looted by thieves long before the archaeologists had a chance to rob them. Carter sent a telegram to the man who was funding his work, Lord Carnarvon. When he arrived from England they found on the door a hieroglyphic inscription warning that the tomb was protected by a curse. Anybody who disturbed the Pharaoh's rest was in for trouble, it said.

Everybody laughed at the superstitious old Egyptians who actually believed in curses. They broke the seals and people entered the Pharaoh's tomb for the first time in 3,279 years.

At which point the curse got them.

As Lord Carnarvon stepped into the tomb, a mosquito bit him. He got sick and died. Carter's partner, Richard Bethell, keeled over a few weeks later. His father, Lord Westbury, committed suicide. Colonel Herbat, who entered the tomb with Carter, died unexpectedly. So did Jonathan Carver, who was also with them.

When they took out Tutankhamun's mummy, they turned it over to Sir Archibald Douglas Reid to be X-rayed. He promptly died too. Even Howard Carter's canary died. It was eaten by a python the day he entered the tomb. The python was Tutankhamun's symbol in Ancient Egypt.

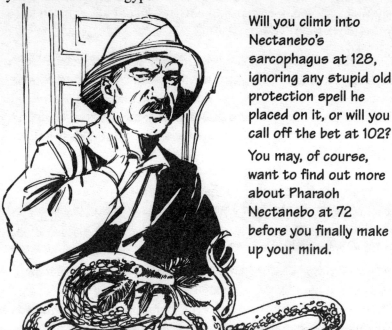

Will you climb into Nectanebo's sarcophagus at 128, ignoring any stupid old protection spell he placed on it, or will you call off the bet at 102?

You may, of course, want to find out more about Pharaoh Nectanebo at 72 before you finally make up your mind.

〈41〉

You assume that if there is an entrance anywhere, it's likely to be some distance above ground, otherwise it would have been found before now. You look at the polished limestone casing of the pyramid and move towards the first tier.

For someone as young, fit and courageous as yourself, climbing the pyramid proves quite possible. But it's slow work, made even slower by the fact you're searching for a hidden entrance.

Eventually, after painstaking examination of every block, you conclude that if the pyramid has an entrance at all, it's not on this face. You climb down, experiencing a mixture of disappointment and determination.

And as you reach the ground again, you're seized by two muscle-bound characters whose dress is Egyptian, but whose features you would swear were definitely Persian.

"Tell us what you've found or have your throat cut!" one hisses viciously in your left ear.

These two Persian clowns have each got 25 Life Points and are carrying +8 daggers. If, despite your valiant efforts, they still kill you, go to 13. If you kill them, you can take the daggers and a handy healing potion worth a double dice roll of restored Life Points, concealed in a kilt. After that, you can search the east face at 25, the west face at 57 or the north face at 68. Or failing that, you can turn back to your map at 103 and select another destination.

search the east face at 25, the west face at 57 or the north face at 68. Or failing that, you can turn back to your map at 103

42

There is a sound like a thunderclap. Your eyes are blinded by a great white light. The world begins to whirl around you as your soul is swept from your body and propelled through a narrow shaft upwards and out of the great stone structure.

You hurtle skywards at escape velocity, up, up, up beyond the very atmosphere and yet your speed does not diminish. Glancing down you realise you can see the curvature of the Earth and in a moment you see your home planet as a vast blue sphere.

And still your journey does not end, for you streak out of the solar system heading for deep space. Your mind dissolves in ecstasy as you travel on, and on, and on, and on ... until ...

You halt. You expand. You combust. You shine. The vast nuclear furnaces within your frame roar and rumble with the fires of heaven as you howl in purest joy.

You might like to know you've gone the way of the old Egyptian Pharaohs who believed that when they died, their souls became one with the great transpolar stars. However, it

means all you can do now is shine for 20,000,000 years or so until you become a Red Giant or White Dwarf or Black Hole – at which point you can crawl back gratefully to 13.

In the mess left by one of the crumbled mummies you notice a neat-looking dagger of volcanic glass. In the mess left by the other, you notice a pellet of metallic antimony which you recognise as a Perpetual Pill. Joyfully you pick both up.

The dagger will kill any single enemy outright on a successful hit. Throw one die to discover how many times you can use it . The Perpetual Pill will restore a double dice roll of Life Points every time you take it, and will reappear (in the natural course of events!) two sections later, ready to be swallowed again. (Although I'd advise you to wipe it carefully before doing so.) Now you can select another destination from 103, or explore this area further at 62.

You find yourself walking down the stately corridors of a mud-brick palace of monumental proportions, over-awed by the sheer opulence of the furnishings, the barbaric splendour of it all. There is gold and lapis, craft works of great ingenuity and style, magnificent hangings, and richly dressed servants everywhere.

"Prepare to meet thy God!" calls an official.

It suddenly occurs to you that this is no death sentence. In Ancient Egypt, God and the Pharaoh were the same person.

You stare down the great hall at the Pharaoh on his throne. Like most of his subjects he's dressed in a linen apron, although he is also wearing headgear that looks like a bishop's mitre doubled. Since you have no more idea of the date than you have how you got here, you wonder which of Egypt's Pharaohs this might be. Since the civilization ran from 3,100 B.C. until 30 B.C., you've a lot to chose from. Your skin prickles at the thought of facing Rameses the Great, who expanded the kingdom so thoroughly. The man on the throne stands up and walks towards you. Those in the chamber prostrate themselves the moment he moves, with the exception of two burly ushers who hurry in front of him calling, "On pain of death, don't touch the Pharaoh!"

He stops before you and, to your astonishment, he holds out his hand. "Hello," he says pleasantly. "My name is Nectanebo."

You're in the time of the Pharaoh whose sarcophagus is in the British Museum! You look at his hand, then glance at the ushers.

Nectanebo smiles. "I'm afraid my subjects are a superstitious lot. They believe that if you touch the Pharaoh, you'll be struck down dead. You'll not be bothered about that since you've come here from the future."

You stare at him, stunned. He knows where you've come from – or at least when you've come from! How? What's going on here?

Never mind that. You've got a Pharaoh waiting to shake your hand. Will you risk it at 28? Or refuse the handshake at 82? Seems a small thing, but your life may well depend on it.

45

You find yourself in a cramped chamber with no apparent exit, and you experience a growing panic until you happen to look up and discover an open trapdoor in the ceiling. With an athletic leap, you manage to catch an edge and pull yourself up into a passageway so narrow you literally have to crawl along it.

As you do so, a faint ringing begins in your ears and a tingling invades the rest of your body.

Sure sign there's ancient magic afoot. It won't kill you, but it will make a difference to where this passage leads. Roll one die. Score 1 and the passage leads to 8; 2 and it goes to 73; 3 and it's 39; 4 and it's 118; 5 and it's 133; 6 and it's 49.

46

The passageway slopes gradually upwards. You follow it until, to your surprise, it ends at what appears to be a blank wall. Then you notice a massive sloping slab which looks as though it was built on a pivot. You try pushing it and, sure enough, the slab rotates, taking a portion of the floor with it and carrying you into a different passageway altogether. You turn, but the slab has locked into place again. It is impossible to open from this side.

Which leaves you with the choice of turning right on the passageway you're now in and going to 61, or turning left and following it to 89.

47

Moving forward again, the passageway does not get any less slippery, but the narrow ramps to each side are now slotted at regular intervals. Since the passageway is less than a metre wide, you can use the slots to give yourself a firm foothold.

Thus, you make your way cautiously along the Grand Gallery and, despite the peril of your position, you cannot but help admire the skill of the Ancient Egyptians. To each side of you the walls rise vertically in seven courses of polished limestone to a total height of nine metres.

After laboriously moving some 50 metres, you reach a massive metre high block of stone, like a step constructed for a giant. You climb on top of it to find yourself standing on a two by two-and-a-half metre platform. Directly in front of you, the ceiling drops to a height of little more than a metre to form what looks like some sort of portcullis opening into a small chamber.

You crouch down to make your way through the opening, but as you step forward, a portcullis slab slams down to block your way. You jump back in alarm, then lean forward again to examine the curious decoration engraved on the surface of the slab.

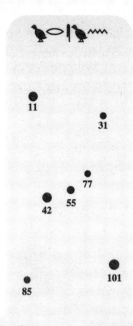

Each of the seven circles between the hieroglyphs glows faintly like a distant star, and as you stare fascinated at the pattern, you experience an irresistible urge to press one of them.

But which one? You seem to be faced with the choice of catapulting yourself to sections 11, 31, 42, 55, 77, 85 or 101 without a single clue as to what might happen to you when you get there. And even as you stand paralysed by indecision, your finger reaches out and presses firmly on ...

The choice, once more, is up to you!

This place is stuffed with goods as well, just like the main chamber. The odd thing is, the stuff is all over the place as if it had just been thrown in like junk, not laid out neatly as you'd expect in a tomb.

You check the walls carefully to see if there's an exit and when you discover there is not, you're about to come out again when you notice several finely-made weapons among the grave goods.

You decide to select a really neat +5 dagger and +7 sword which you stick into your belt before returning to the main chamber.

Let's hope you get a chance to use them. For the moment, all you can do is explore the ascending passage at 24 or climb back into the sarcophagus (yuk!) at 63.

Although this is the smallest of the three great pyramids, it's still enormous by any normal standards. Flicking through your *Brief History of Ancient Egypt,* you discover that this is referred to as the Pyramid of Mykerinos, built by a Pharaoh the Egyptians actually called Menkaura.

Could this structure contain the treasure Nectanebo seeks?

Only one way to find out and that's to get searching for a secret entrance. You can examine the north face at 37, the south face at 65, the east face at 74 or the west face at 145.

You push the door and step cautiously into a narrow cramped stone chamber beyond. Then you freeze as a massive cobra rises up directly in front of you, its head drawn back ready to strike. You realise at once that if a snake this size gets in even a single strike against you, the venom will kill you outright.

What to do? If you turn back now, you're likely to be trapped in that maze of passageways, although you can risk it, if you want, at 29. Your other option is to fight the cobra at 70.

With a scream of terror, you plunge into ... a shallow pit – for the loss of 0.05 of a Life Point! (If this kills you, go to 13.)

You lie for a moment catching your breath. Then you notice an opening in the ceiling. It seems to be the entrance to a near vertical shaft that bores upwards through the pyramid.

If you want to ignore this shaft, continue down the descending passage to 34, or return to take the ascending passage near the entrance at 18, or go to 103 and select another destination. But if you want to climb into the narrow shaft, you're into another Absolutely Anything Roll. Should this kill you, turn to 13. Should it fail, you're stuck with 34, 18 or 103. But should it succeed ... your joy will be boundless (probably) as you haul yourself into the narrow shaft at 90.

You walk a little hesitantly into the workshops of the embalmers. There is a strong smell of bitter aloes in the air. A corpse is stretched out naked on a table, gazing sightlessly at the ceiling.

"He's a noble," your gloomy companion explains, "so he will naturally receive the best treatment available. Ah, here come my professional colleagues now."

Two even more gloomy looking individuals walk solemnly into the chamber and stare down sorrowfully at the corpse. You watch with horrified fascination as one of the embalmers splits the corpse's nose and inserts a tube up it. His companion begins to pour some foul-smelling fluid into it from a ceramic jar.

"They are introducing solvents into the skull cavity," your companion explains. "When the brain has partly liquefied, they will draw it out through the nostrils with an iron hook."

One of the embalmers shoves an iron hook up the poor fellow's nose. There is a liquid squelching, plopping, sound and you look away hurriedly, but not hurriedly enough to miss catching sight of runny grey matter emerging from the nostril.

"Now they'll call the dissector," says the embalmer.

You turn back again in time to see a third, very plump, man join the other two. He is carrying an enormous stone-bladed knife.

"It's made from Ethiopian stone." explains your companion. "Nothing else is sharp enough."

The plump man nods briefly to the other two, then leans over the corpse. He makes a long deep incision across the abdomen. Then, to your astonishment, he turns and runs.

To your even greater astonishment, the two dignified embalmers race after him, hurling stones and abuse.

"What?" you ask. "What's going on? What did he do wrong?"

Your companion shakes his head mournfully. "They're chasing him because of the injury he's just done to their client. Once he's been chased, he can get on with the job."

Despite yourself, you're developing a horrid fascination for this grisly business. You watch as between them the embalmers and dissector remove the entrails of the corpse, and drop them steaming into the nearest canopic jar.

"They'll be buried with him, of course," your companion says. "Can't go off to the Underworld without your insides, can you?"

You don't answer, mainly because you are fighting not to throw up. As you fight the nausea, the men flush out the abdomen with palm wine and stuff scented aloes in the bowel cavity.

"That's about all you can see for now," your companion says. "They'll soak the body in a solution of natron salts for seventy days then bandage it to make the mummy. This creates a suitable vehicle for his Ka should it ever wish again to walk on earth, although I've often wondered what sort of life you would lead without your bowels or brains, and your backside full of aloes."

You push past him, desperate to get into the open air.

Frankly this is such a traumatic experience that you'd best throw two dice to find out whether or not you survive it. Score 12 and the shock kills you, in which case write a quick will telling them to leave your corpse alone and go to 13. But with any other score you survive, at least long enough to get to 59.

53

The passageway continues to slope downwards and now your eyes have grown accustomed to the gloom, you can see reasonably well.

Or at least well enough to stop yourself walking into the enormous granite slab which is blocking the passageway ahead. You lean forward with a sinking heart to try to read the hieroglyphs incised upon it:

If you are able to follow the instructions, you will discover the stone slides back with a grinding noise, leaving you free to proceed to 106. If not, you could try to find the item mentioned in the inscription; or search the eastern face of the pyramid at 25, the south face at 41, the west face at 57, for another entrance, or go back to your map at 103.

You remove your shoes and hand them across. The little man gives you a folded piece of papyrus and makes a run for it.

You unfold the papyrus. It shows a diagrammatic cross-section of the pyramid under which you're standing.

You look at it with a mixture of irritation and delight. The map shows secret entrances and chambers – but no indication of north, south, east or west! You begin to walk around the pyramid. Since one of the secret entrances is supposed to be at ground level, you concentrate on finding that one first. All the stones look completely solid and you feel a total idiot trying to give them a quarter turn anti-clockwise. But then, suddenly, one actually moves!

For a moment you stand staring, hardly able to believe your luck. The stone definitely moved. You reach forward and prod it experimentally. At once the stone tilts on its axis, revealing a downward sloping passage.

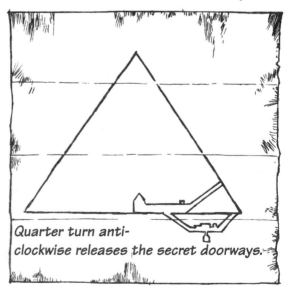

Quarter turn anti-clockwise releases the secret doorways.

Excitedly you start to climb the sloping side in the hope of finding the second entrance which, according to your map, is just above the first. In moments you've discovered that as well. Now you know both secret entrances into the Khefra pyramid. And both lead to downward-sloping passageways.

Will you take secret entrance number 1 at ground level by turning to 21, or would you prefer the higher entrance at 36?

There is a sound like a thunderclap. Your eyes are blinded by a great white light. The world begins to whirl around you as your soul is swept from your body and propelled through a narrow shaft upwards and out of the great stone structure.

A moment of confusion as the world spins around you, then you find yourself dropping like a stone ... all the way into Nectanebo's sarcophagus in the British Museum.

Oh no, you've been caught up in a time warp! You're all the way back to 128 and your memory's fading fast. Nothing for it but to fight your way through this whole mess again. Roll one die. Score 1, 2 or 3 and go to 86. Score 4 , 5 or 6 and go to 144.

Nope, it's locked tight.

And since the wall's too high to climb, your only way to go is into that dimly-lit building at 115.

You assume that if there is an entrance anywhere, it's likely to be some distance above ground, otherwise it would have been found before now. You look at the polished limestone casing of the pyramid and move towards the first tier.

For someone as young, fit and courageous as yourself, climbing the pyramid proves quite possible. But it's slow work, made even slower by the fact you're searching for a hidden entrance.

Eventually, after painstaking examination of every block, you conclude that if the pyramid has an entrance at all, it's not on this face. You climb down, experiencing a mixture of disappointment and determination.

But as you reach the ground again, you're seized by two muscle-bound characters whose dress is Egyptian, but whose features you would swear were definitely Persian.

"Tell us what you've found or we'll cut your throat!" one hisses viciously in your left ear.

These two Persian clowns have each got 30 Life Points and are carrying +10 throat cutting equipment in the form of daggers. If, despite your most valiant efforts, they still kill you, go to 13. If you kill them, you can take the daggers and a handy poison stiletto, concealed in a dangerous manner in one of their kilts: a single prick means instant death to one opponent. (Roll one die to see how many times you can use the stiletto before the poison runs out.)

After that, you can search the south face at 41, the east face at 25 or the north face at 68. Or failing that, you can turn back to your map at 103 and select another destination.

The foreman Khonsu stares down at the body of Eye-Gor, then frowns at you. "That was a very good workman you just bashed," he says.

"He was trying to kill me!" you protest.

"I know," nods Khonsu. "All the same, I won't get much work out of him now, will I? I think I might want a bit extra on our deal for the tablet by way of compensation."

"How much extra?" you ask, appalled.

Khonsu says. "We'll make it two statues of Bastet, shall we?"

If you happen to have two statues of Bastet about your person, you can complete the deal at 155.

If not, your only choices are to fight Khonsu as well at 88 or give up on the tablet deal altogether and return to 103 where you can select another destination.

Leaving Funeral Street (gratefully) behind, you turn into the main thoroughfare that crosses the city. And walk straight into a pair of ugly looking guards!

They cry in unison. "That's the one God's been looking for!"

Back to God again, by the looks of things. If you're fed up running, you can go with them directly to 44. But if your stubborn streak is playing up, there's always ultra-violence to fall back on. Each guard has 35 Life Points (count 'em!) and carries a +10 sword. If by some miracle you slaughter them, you can collect your just reward at 149, if not, go to 13.

60

You are astonished at how well-engineered this corridor is – how beautifully cut the paving slabs – but your astonishment turns to outright awe when the corridor opens into the courtyard of a huge temple hewn from the bedrock beneath the sphinx.

Beyond the broad sweep of the courtyard rise four gigantic seated statues flanking an enormous entrance door. You pass through it into a massive hallway, and you are drawn forward to the opening to an inner shrine. There is some sort of crystal substance embedded in the walls so that the tiny light of your oil lamp is magnified a thousand times, allowing you to see almost as clearly as you would in daylight. In the precise centre of the shrine is a stone altar table, beyond which stands a massive statue of the god Osiris. On the altar is a jewel-encrusted flail.

You take a step inside and at once a massive stone slab plummets down behind you, sealing you into the shrine. You swing round in alarm and push against the slab, but it is absolutely immovable. As you step back in despair, you notice several curious symbols cut into its surface:

They are like no hieroglyph you have ever seen.

And yet they may still be of some assistance to you. If they are, follow instructions. If not, the bad news is the oil in your lamp eventually gives out and you're stuck in the darkness of this subterranean temple until starvation carries you to 13.

You follow the passageway only a short distance before you reach a dead end. Your way has been blocked by a massive granite slab inscribed with a tight mass of delicately cut hieroglyphs. With some difficulty you translate the glyphs, which form an intriguing message:

Oh wanderer, to pass safely beyond this barrier of stone, pronounce clearly the name given to this mystic symbol *– select from the names bennu, scarab or ankh.*

Mystic symbol my eye – it looks like some sort of bug. But since this is obviously a magical lock, it looks like you have to pick one of the names if you want to get past. If you think the correct name is bennu, turn to 69. If you think it's scarab, turn to 94. If you consider it might be ankh, turn to 84.

After nearly an hour, you have searched the area thoroughly and are now facing a doorway in one of the mastabas that seems to have been forced open recently. You step across the threshold and are almost blinded by a sudden light as the most beautiful woman you have ever seen appears in mid-air beyond the central altar.

"I am Isis," she smiles. "I have been following your progress with great interest and I have decided to give you a gift." She waves a casual hand and two small items appear on the altar. One is a purple scarab, the other an equally purple orb. "You may have one or the other of these two items, but you may not have both."

"What do they do, Your Isisness?" you ask.

"You will learn that when you have chosen," Isis tells you.

No arguing with a goddess. So make your choice of the purple scarab at 114 or the purple orb at 139.

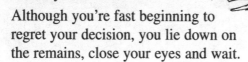

Holding your nose against the smell, you climb back into the sarcophagus. As you step onto the mummy's chest, there is a dry, crunching sound and your foot goes all the way through. You free your leg and the mummy's head falls off.

Although you're fast beginning to regret your decision, you lie down on the remains, close your eyes and wait.

While you're waiting, it might be a good idea to make an Absolutely Anything Roll. If the roll kills you, it means that the mummy comes to life and strangles you for breaking off its head, in which case go to 13. If the roll succeeds, you'll open your eyes to find yourself climbing back into Nectanebo's sarcophagus at 128. If it fails, you'll have to apologise to the mummy and climb out again to explore the ante-chamber at 48 or the passageway at 24.

This is sort of weird. There's frenzied activity going on right in the shadow of the Great Pyramid as teams of workmen labour to fill in two immense pits. At the bottom of each you can see an enormous wooden boat.

You blink. Maybe you got this wrong. Those boats are far too large to sail the Nile, but what would sea-going vessels be doing here on the edge of the desert? All the same, they're definitely boats and they're definitely enormous, and they're definitely being buried by the workmen.

"What's going on here?" you ask curiously.

"Pharaoh's orders," the foreman tells you with a sniff. "We dug these up while we were looking for the treasure of the pyramids.

Pharaoh's got everybody looking for the treasure of the pyramids these days – he'll get you at it if you're not careful. Anyway, we dug up these old ships, but there was no treasure – only other thing we found was a little old clay tablet with some funny signs on it."

"What happened to the clay tablet?" you ask.

"I kept it," says the foreman. "I want to exchange it for a little statue of Bastet to put in my shrine at home."

If you happen to have a little statue of Bastet about your person you can exchange it for the mysterious tablet at 148. If not, your only choice is to return to your map at 103 and select another destination.

Nope, no secret entrance here.

You can examine the north face at 37, the east face at 74 or the west face at 145. Or if you get bored with the whole thing, you can always go back to 103 and select another destination from your map.

66

No sooner have the names passed your lips than your head explodes.

Clean up the mess and go to 13.

67

You are admiring a bas-relief of Anubis, the jackal god of the Underworld, when you realise everything has suddenly gone quiet. A quick glance tells you a miracle has happened. Apart from yourself, this gallery of the Egyptian Rooms is empty! Quick as boiled asparagus, you nip back to the sarcophagus of Nectanebo. It's empty, of course, because for some reason this old Pharaoh was never actually buried in it. Which was what prompted Spider Simpson to bet you a year's supply of toffee apples you wouldn't hide inside it and stay there one whole night.

You are about to climb into the sarcophagus when a neatly framed notice catches your eye. Even though someone may come in at any moment, you bend down to read it. It's a translation of the sarcophagus hieroglyphs – or some of them at least. The translation reads:

> I, Nectanebo, Pharaoh of the Two Lands,
> whom men call wizard, have placed upon my sarcophagus a
> powerful spell of protection which will carry off anyone who
> despoils my property.

You straighten up to think.

As well you might. There are a lot of people who believe the old Pharaohs really could work magic – look what happened when they opened Tutankhamun's tomb. At the same time, a year's supply of toffee apples isn't to be sneezed at. So do you take the risk of hiding in the sarcophagus at 128? Or would you prefer to race to 102 and tell Spider you've changed your mind?

Then again, would you be interested in finding out what really DID happen when they opened Tutankhamun's tomb at 40?

You assume that if there is an entrance anywhere, it's likely to be some distance above ground, otherwise it would have been found before now. You look at the polished limestone casing of the pyramid and move towards the first tier.

For someone as young, fit and courageous as yourself, climbing the pyramid proves quite possible. But it's slow work, made even slower by the fact you're searching for a hidden entrance.

Eventually, after painstaking examination of every block, you conclude that if the pyramid has an entrance at all, it's not on this face. You climb down, experiencing a mixture of disappointment and determination, when suddenly an enormous counterbalanced slab turns inwards, revealing a dark passageway leading downwards into the gloomy bowels of the pyramid.

Spooky. If you want to explore that passageway, turn to 87. If you don't, you can always see if there's a better option on the eastern face at 25, the south face at 41, or the west face at 57. You can even get off the pyramid altogether by sliding back down to your map at 103 and selecting another destination.

Feeling a bit of a prat, you pronounce the name aloud. The sound reverberates in the enclosed space and at once you experience the unmistakable tingle that tells you there's magic about.

You look expectantly at the slab. There is a low grinding noise like the sound of stone on stone.

Followed by a low splatting noise as an enormous block drops from the ceiling to squash you flat. Go to 13.

70

Cautiously you move towards the great snake. Which has only 30 Life Points, but merely needs one successful strike to kill you. However, the Osiris Flail you're carrying has a magical charge that makes it a deadly weapon when used against a single opponent. Like the cobra, the flail kills instantly, so you only have to get in one successful strike. Unfortunately this mighty weapon is very old, so you'll need to roll a die to find out how many times you can use it before the charge runs out. If the cobra kills you, go to 13. If you kill the cobra, take the exit door to your right and turn to 45.

You find yourself standing at the mouth of a horizontal passageway, to one side of which are what appear to be joist holes in the wall. Behind you is a descending passage. Almost at your feet is a narrow shaft that plunges straight down towards the bedrock below the massive pyramid.

To negotiate that shaft, go to 76. For the horizontal passage go to 129, or you can examine the joist holes at 14. Or you can take the descending passage to leave the pyramid and return to your map at 103 to select another destination.

Back in 380 B.C. an army general called Nectanebo grabbed the throne and founded the 30th Dynasty. His son Tachos took over from him in 365 B.C. and later launched an invasion of Palestine aided by Agesilaus, the King of Sparta. Unfortunately the two of them fell out, Agesilaus withdrew funding and Tachos tried to raise the readies by imposing heavy taxes.

The Ancient Egyptians didn't like being taxed any more than we do and fell in behind Tachos' nephew when he made a bid for the throne. Tachos' nephew was Nectanebo II. He was the last of the native Egyptian kings. He reigned from 360 to 343 B.C. – Agesilaus liked him better than his uncle and gave him lots of encouragement and support.

But if Nectanebo II had no trouble with Agesilaus, he had a lot of trouble with Artaxerxes III who was King of Persia at the time. The two were always squaring up to one another.

So. Will you risk Nectanebo's curse by climbing into the sarcophagus at 128, or will you forget the whole thing at 102?

⟨73⟩

You find yourself north of the Great Sphinx in the midst of a group of stone mastabas. These rectangular superstructures have sides constructed in the form of panelled niches painted white and decorated with elaborate matting designs. You are wondering whether you should try searching each of them when

a curious shuffling sound behind you causes you to turn around
– just in time to see three animated mummies bearing down on
you, with murderous expressions on their faces.

**How on earth can you tell the expressions on their faces when
they're swathed in bandages? But never mind that now. Unless
you want to tackle these three Egyptian stooges, you'd better
head off to 103 as fast as your legs can carry you. But if you
do feel like (yet another) fight, it's all yours at 27.**

Nope, no secret entrance here.

**You can examine the south face at 65, the north face at 37 or
the west face at 145. Or you can always go back to 103 and
select another destination from your map ...**

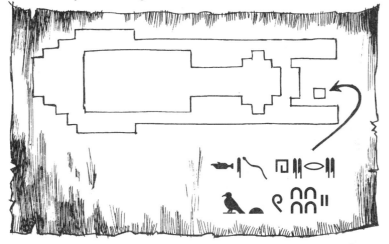

The papyrus is torn and faded, as if it had lain buried in the sand
for a very long time – although you would imagine burying
papyrus in the sand for a very long time would destroy it
altogether. But while the drawing is crudely done, you have no
real difficulty in making it out.

**If this isn't helpful, your only options are a return to 4 for
further searching, or to 103 to select another destination.**

You squeeze your way into the narrow shaft and immediately feel a dice roll coming on.

As well you might since your chances of negotiating this shaft all the way to the bottom depend entirely on the results of an Absolutely Anything Roll. If the roll kills you, go to 13. If it fails, you'd better climb out of the shaft and make up your mind whether you want to take the horizontal passage at 129. Or you could try the descending passage which will eventually get you out of the pyramid altogether, so you can return to your map at 103 and select another destination. (Or back here again, if you want another try.) If it succeeds – the Absolutely Anything Roll, that is, since you've probably forgotten by now – you'll emerge at 98.

⟨ 77 ⟩

For a moment nothing happens. There is such silence that you can actually hear your heart beating. Then, with no more than a whisper, the slab withdraws. You step forward into a small ante-chamber which allows you to stand upright. You look around. There is only one exit from this chamber, but it too is closed off by an inscribed slab. With a distinct feeling of déjà vu, you lean forward to examine the markings.

To your absolute astonishment, they're in English:

If Mykerinos is really Menkaura, press the sign of the ankh, unless Khefra was the son of Khufu, in which case press the sign of the scarab. Get this wrong and you die.
Signed, a Well-wisher.

Beneath the inscription are two symbols – a 🪲 and a ☥ .

Press the 🪲 and go to 126. Press the ☥ and go to 120.

⟨ 78 ⟩

"Oh, no I won't!" you yell in true pantomime fashion and hurl yourself violently upon them.

Which is where, I have to tell you, things get complicated. First off, each of these three closely-shaven gents sports 50 Life Points and carries a +5 dagger, but for once in a game book that's not really important, because for every one of them you manage to kill, another two will pile in through the hole from outside. This is bad news, because it means there's absolutely no way you can win this fight, thus pleasing those interfering old busybodies who keep saying there's too much violence in solo adventures.

On the other hand, the baldies will do their level best to knock you unconscious by bringing your Life Points below five. If they do, they'll revive you and drag you off to 136.

But on the third hand, trying to bring somebody's Life Points below five can quite often accidentally bring them down to zero. If this happens to you, go to 13.

You make for the exit corridor as fast as your legs will carry you, but unfortunately that doesn't seem to be nearly fast enough. There is a hideous crash behind you and you turn to find the sarcophagus shattered, the mummy case open and the mummy inside lumbering towards you like something from a late-night TV re-run of an old Boris Karloff movie.

"Just where do you think you're going?" it asks in a voice that reminds you of a headmaster speaking from the bottom of an empty swimming pool.
"I want the Eye of Horus!"

If you can give this animated corpse the Eye of Horus, for heaven's sake do so and make a break down that exit corridor to 60. If you can't, I'm afraid you're in for a fight and a pretty big one. The mummy has a massive 130 Death Points (which function exactly like Life Points) and a Wizened Hand which will kill you instantly if it happens to throw a double six during combat. What's more, although unarmed (one of them fell off, heh-heh) it still strikes with all the force of a +10 sword, due to its supernatural undead strength. If, as seems increasingly likely, you are killed in this encounter, turn to 13. Should you miraculously survive, you can limp to 60.

There is a tiny dust-storm in the distance as the little man barrels at high speed across the desert sands, not realising you aren't following. You glare at the retreating figure, but a part of you is intrigued: in trying to sell you the map, the little man gave you quite a lot of information. One entrance at ground level, the other directly above it. A quarter twist to open the secret doors.

You decide to concentrate on finding the ground level entrance, moving round the pyramid one stone at a time and trying each one with a quarter twist. All the stones look completely solid but you try anyway. It takes far longer than you would ever have imagined, but suddenly a stone moves!

It doesn't move much. In fact it moves so little that you wonder if it might have been your imagination. But you're sufficiently encouraged to reach forward and prod it. At once the stone tilts on its axis, revealing a downward sloping passage.

Excitedly you start to climb the sloping side in the hope of finding the second entrance which, according to the little man, is just above the first. In moments you've discovered that as well. Now you know both secret entrances into the Khefra pyramid. And both lead to downward-sloping passageways.

So do you plan to take the secret entrance at ground level by turning to 21, or would you prefer the higher entrance at 36? The choice, as always, is yours.

No sooner have the names passed your lips than your head explodes.

Clean up the mess and go to 13.

You pointedly ignore the proffered hand and turn away. At once the ushers begin a wailing cry. "The Pharaoh is insulted! The Pharaoh is insulted!"

An enormously muscled Egyptian clumps into the chamber, carrying a club. He walks up to the Pharaoh and bows.

Nectanebo sighs, then turns to you. "I'm afraid it's the custom that if you insult the Pharaoh, even accidentally, you must fight the King's Champion. I do apologise."

You turn to look again at the King's Champion with his bulging muscles, his thick neck and his wicked club.

"I don't have to fight him?" you gasp.

Oh yes, you do. And the bad news is that the K.C. has 70 Life Points and his muscles are so thick they work exactly like -5 armour, deducting five points from every damage score against him. His club does +10 damage and ... you have to fight him to the death! If you die, go to 13. If he dies, go to 111.

You find yourself in the midst of a group of regularly laid stone mastabas, just west of the Great Pyramid. These rectangular superstructures have sides constructed in the form of panelled niches, painted white and decorated with elaborate matting designs. There is a little niche chapel set into the side of one close by you, and you can see an electrum ankh just inside, presumably left as an offering to the gods.

It's probably cursed, but if you want to risk it, you can take the ankh at 109. Otherwise you can return to your map at 103 and select another destination.

Feeling a bit of a prat, you pronounce the name aloud. The sound reverberates in the enclosed space, and at once you experience the unmistakable tingle that tells you there's magic about. You look expectantly at the slab. There is a low grinding noise like the sound of stone on stone.

Followed by a low splatting noise as an enormous block drops from the ceiling to squash you flat. Go to 13.

85

There is a sound like a thunderclap. Your eyes are blinded by a great white light. The world begins to whirl around you as your soul is swept from your body and propelled through a narrow shaft upwards and out of the great stone structure.

You hurtle skywards at escape velocity, up, up, up beyond the very atmosphere, and yet your speed does not diminish. Glancing down you realise you can see the curvature of the Earth and in a moment you see your home planet as a vast blue sphere.

And still your journey does not end, for you streak out of the solar system heading for deep space. Your mind dissolves in ecstasy as you travel on, and on, and on, and on, and on ... until ...

You halt. You expand. You combust. You shine. The vast nuclear furnaces within your frame roar and rumble with the fires of heaven as you howl in purest joy.

You might like to know you've gone the way of the old Egyptian Pharaohs, who believed that when they died, their souls migrated heavenwards to become one with the great transpolar stars. Quite an experience you must agree, but it means all you can do now is shine for 20,000,000 years or so until you become a Red Giant or White Dwarf or Black Hole, at which point you can crawl back gratefully to 13.

Your eyes open abruptly of their own accord. It's daylight, so you've obviously slept soundly right through the night. A bubble of delight pops pleasantly inside your head. Boy, will Spider Simpson be annoyed! Now all you have to do is climb out of the sarcophagus and –

You're not in the sarcophagus!

You look around. You're not in the British Museum! You're in some sort of huge open courtyard and an early morning sun is burning down from a sky that looks as if it hasn't seen a cloud in fifty years.

You're not even in London!!

This is impossible. But it's happened. Unless, of course, you're dreaming. You clamber to your feet. The courtyard is paved with hard stone slabs covered in a noticeable sprinkling of dust and fine sand. To your right and to your left are colonnades of gigantic pillars, each carved to represent a standing figure. From your tour of the British Museum, you recognise the figure as Osiris, king of the dead. The carvings show him in the wrappings of a mummy, his arms crossed on his chest, his hands holding crook and flail.

Behind you is a massive pylon gateway, closed off by an immense wooden door. Before you is a broad, shallow flight of worn stone steps ending in an open doorway to a dimly-lit building beyond. Somehow none of this feels like a dream.

Dream or not, what are you going to do about it? You can try the wooden door behind you at 56. Or investigate that dimly-lit building at 115.

87

Bravely you plunge into the sloping passage. And stop dead as a Persian dagger pricks your throat. "So," hisses a voice out of the darkness, "one of Nectanebo's people has finally found us!"

Bravely you wonder if you should turn and run.

If you do (turn and run that is) you're entitled to search the eastern face of the pyramid at 25, the south face at 41, or the west face at 57, although you might be safer running all the way to 103 and selecting a new destination from your map. Alternatively, you might want to risk a fight here, but risk it certainly will be, because you can't see how many opponents you might be facing in this dark passage. So if you do decide to fight, first throw one die. This will tell you how many foes you face. Each has 20 Life Points and carries a +5 dagger. Should he/they kill you, turn to 13. If you manage to dispatch him/them, you can collect from each corpse a healing potion worth a double dice roll of Life Points and follow the passage down to 53.

88

"A deal's a deal," you growl, "and we had a deal!"

With which you launch a surprise attack.

Which sneaky move gives you first strike without having to roll dice for it. And probably just as well since Khonsu has an amazing 75 Life Points due to lots of fresh air and physical activity. What's more, he's carrying a +5 dagger in his tool kit. If you survive this fight, you can collect your tablet (if nothing else goes wrong) at 155. If you don't, you've got nowhere to turn but 13.

You step from the passageway into a large, plain chamber with a vaulted ceiling. Once again you are struck by the astonishing engineering skills of the Ancient Egyptians, for these great stones have held back time for centuries.

But your heart leaps as you catch sight of a stone sarcophagus near the northern wall of the chamber. This may be what you're looking for – the receptacle of the treasure and marvellous artefacts that Nectanebo wants.

You move to throw the sarcophagus lid aside, but it is firmly fixed. A hieroglyphic inscription on the lid (which you can now translate with ease) reads:

To open, invoke the deity of war.

Below it is a painting of the god Osiris flanked by the goddess Isis on his right and the goddess Sekhmet on his left. Quite clearly, the 'deity of war' must be one of these.

To invoke Osiris, turn to 130; Isis, turn to 141; Sekhmet, turn to 154.

You haul yourself up into the narrow shaft with a boundless feeling of joy which lasts until you realise what sort of a mess you've got yourself into. The shaft is so narrow you can't see where you're going, it's so airless you're in danger of suffocation, and so steep you're in grave danger of falling. What's more, short of dropping like a stone, there's no way for you to get back.

If you decide to drop like a stone, make an Absolutely Anything Roll. If this kills you, go to 13. If the roll succeeds, you can continue down the descending passage to 34, or return to the ascending passage near the entrance at 18, or leave the pyramid altogether and select another destination at 103. If the roll fails, you're stuck in the shaft where you can throw one die. Score 1 or 2 and you suffocate and go to 13. Score 3 or 4 and you fall as you near the top, plunging to your death and arriving at 13 with a truly disgusting splatting noise. Score 5 or 6 and you'll eventually haul yourself out of this nightmare at 119.

"Get lost," you tell him politely. "I don't believe in magic."

"Really?" says the jeweller, turning his head-dress back to front and pointing at you with the little finger and forefinger of his left hand.

At once you start to feel odd. A boil pops out suddenly (and painfully) on the end of your nose. You go deaf in your left ear. Your right foot begins to walk around your left foot, turning your legs into corkscrews. You get spots before your eyes and your nose begins to drip.

"There he is!" calls a familiar voice, and a party of shaven priests and armed guards surround you. There is a thumping in your head, a bad taste in your mouth, a crawling all over your skin, a ringing in your ears and a foul smell in your nose as you are dragged to your feet.

Looks like you've just got a taste of an Egyptian curse (again). You can only hope it will all wear off by the time the guards drag you off to 44.

You find yourself in the midst of a group of stone mastabas laid in a regular pattern just across the way from the Great Sphinx. These rectangular buildings have sides constructed in the form of panelled niches, are painted white, and are decorated with elaborate matting designs.

"Used to bury the nobles here," says a voice behind you. You turn to find yourself staring into the twinkling eyes of a little wizened man who looks somehow vaguely familiar.

"Want to buy a statue of Bastet?" he asks cheerfully. "You can have it in exchange for an electrum ankh. Not interested in any other sort."

If you want to buy a statue of the cat goddess Bastet (little bit of extra information there) and happen to have an electrum ankh, you can do so at 146. If you don't or you haven't, get back to your map at 103 and select another destination.

You shrug. "I think I must have been dreaming," you tell him. "It's the only logical explanation."

"Isn't logic a bummer?" Spider remarks.

And you walk out of the Museum onto the rain-swept street and into an utterly boring (but completely logical) future.

Feeling a bit of a prat, you pronounce the name aloud. The sound reverberates in the enclosed space and at once you experience the unmistakable tingle that tells you there's magic about.

You look expectantly at the slab. There is a low grinding noise like the sound of stone on stone.

At which the slab retracts, leaving you free to proceed out of the pyramid to 103 where you can select another destination.

⟨95⟩

The pit is about four metres deep and seems to be filled with rubble which is piled so high in parts that you should be able to drop down onto it without too much difficulty.

You can do this at 117. On the other hand, you can ignore this little diversion and head for the exit passage at 107, or even retrace your steps all the way up the descending passage to the junction with the ascending passage at 18, or leave the pyramid altogether to select another destination from 103.

You scream and shout and beat your head violently against the blank wall, which pays no attention to you whatsoever. Suddenly you hear a dull thudding noise from somewhere behind the wall. You stop your wailing and listen. A piece of plaster cracks, then falls. Hurriedly you scramble away from the wall – and only just in time, since it crumbles abruptly and caves inwards in a cloud of dust and rubble.

"By Thoth, he's still alive!" you hear a voice cry out in a strange archaic language which, somehow, you understand. "We must have buried him before he was completely dead!"

"Don't be daft," exclaims a second voice, "we removed his intestines and his brain, and stuffed his backside full of aloes before we buried him. If he wasn't dead before then, he certainly was afterwards."

"Just a moment," puts in yet another voice.
"That's not the noble Sen-Nefer! Doesn't look like him, doesn't dress like him, isn't even the same age as him. That's somebody else altogether!"

At which three completely hairless men leap through the hole in the newly collapsed wall and glare at you.

"You'd better come with us, you young grave robber!" one of them growls.

An interesting suggestion, but do you really want to stroll off peacefully with these three baldies? If you do, then turn to 136. On the other hand, if you fancy your chances of fighting your way past the goons and making a break for it, turn to 78.

97

There is a grinding noise as the slab retracts and a massive stone ball rolls towards you. You run, but a second stone slab drops down, sealing the corridor behind you. You try to climb above the path of the oncoming ball, but to your horror, you see that the ceiling is descending, and will soon crush you flat.

You attempt to find your way to 13, and succeed admirably!

98

You emerge from the shaft and drop down without injury into a shallow depression in the floor of a descending passageway. You look both ways as you try to decide what to do next.

Which amounts to going down the passage to 34, or up the passage to where it joins with an ascending passage near the entrance at 18. Or you can return to your map at 103 and select another destination.

99

The Rosetta Stone turns out to be a boring block of black basalt with a lot of obscure ancient writing cut into it. But underneath, the Museum authorities have placed a notice that tells you why it's so important.

The stone was found in 1799 by a group of Napoleon's soldiers and later taken to the British Museum. The writing on it was in two languages, Egyptian and Greek. The Egyptian bit was written twice and one of the versions was in hieroglyphics. In 1822, the French scholar Jean François Champollion finally used the Greek, which he spoke like a native, to figure out the hieroglyphics, which nobody had been able to read for over 2,000 years.

You're sinking into a pool of molten jelly at the tedium of it all when your eye catches a second notice beside the first. This one is headed:

HIEROGLYPHS FOR BEGINNERS
Or How To Write Secret Messages and Mystify Your Friends

This looks a lot more interesting, so you squat down and read it thoroughly.

Hieroglyphics, it says, is a form of writing complicated by the fact that some of the signs stand for whole words, while others stand for letters of the alphabet and numbers. Beginners in the language can start by learning a few of the numbers and the hieroglyphic alphabet. This won't let them translate every Ancient Egyptian inscription they come across, but it can be a great help in certain situations. The notice then goes on:

Here's the number 1   I
This is 10   ∩
And this is 100   ϙ

You can get every number up to 1,000 out of these three because the Ancient Egyptians just repeated them when they wanted to write any higher numbers.

So when you want to write 2, you just go II
For 3 you go III. *And so on.*

It's the same for 10s and 100s.
When you want 20, you write ∩∩
Or you can put one under the other like this: ∩∩ *if you think it looks better.*

For 25, you'd write ∩∩ III II

For 125, you'd just stick the 100 sign in front like this: ϙ ∩∩ III II

So to work out any number, just count the bits and add them together.

To translate inscriptions, it's useful to learn the hieroglyphic alphabet:

=A   =B   =C or K   =CH   =D

=E   =F or PH or V   =G or J   =H   =I or Y

=L or R   =M   =N   =O or U or W

=P   =Q   =S   =SH   =T

=TH   =X   =Z

Although accurate as far as it goes, this is a simplified version that doesn't take into account the way some English letters sound different in different words. The letter C, for example, sounds different in the word 'cake' to the way it does in the word 'nice.'

There's enough shown above to let you translate most of the hieroglyphics you're likely to meet in the average adventure, and more than enough to write secret messages. But remember, the Ancient Egyptians sometimes shortened words for simplicity – so while they sound fine, they may not be spelled exactly the way we spell them.
Signed, the Curator.

That Curator seems a very nice man. Pity he didn't mention how you tell L from R when they're both represented by the same hieroglyph. Or O from U or W, come to that. Probably you're expected to make an intelligent guess. Now you'd better get back to 1 and the rest of your adventure before you seize up with cramp ...

You bend over the sarcophagus. The mummy case inside is
superbly made from sycamore with gold leaf inlay, and somehow
manages to look as new as the day it was carried into this ancient
chamber. Curiously you reach down to discover the case opens
easily – and find an intact mummy inside!

The bandaging is superb, but for some reason a portion of the
face has been left uncovered! You can see leathery skin, closed
eyes and thin, cruel lips drawn back to reveal powerful teeth
locked in the rictus smile of death. There is a tiny ankh key
hanging from a golden chain around its neck.

You stand by that ancient sarcophagus, when the mummy
reaches up and takes you by the throat. Its eyes flicker open.
"Have you got the Eye of Horus?" it asks you hoarsely. "If you
have, give it to me and I'll let you out of here alive. If you
haven't, take the ankh key from round my neck. It will allow you
to return the way you came and open the slab trapdoor at the top
of the steps."

If you happen to be carrying the Eye of Horus, give it to the
mummy and run for the exit corridor at 60. If you don't, then
take that little ankh key and head back the way you came to
103 where you can pick another destination.

There is a sound like a thunderclap. Your eyes are blinded by a
great white light. The world begins to whirl around you as your
soul is swept from your body and propelled through a narrow
shaft upwards and out of the great stone structure.

You hurtle skywards at escape velocity, up, up, up beyond the
very atmosphere and yet your speed does not diminish. Glancing
down you realise you can see the curvature of the Earth and in a
moment you see your home planet as a vast blue sphere.

And still your journey does not end, for you streak out of the
solar system heading for deep space. Your mind dissolves in
ecstasy as you travel on, and on, and on, and on, and on ...

Until ...

You halt. You expand.
You combust. You shine.
The vast nuclear
furnaces within your
frame roar and rumble
with the fires of
heaven as you howl
in purest joy.

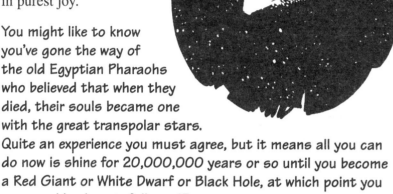

You might like to know
you've gone the way of
the old Egyptian Pharaohs
who believed that when they
died, their souls became one
with the great transpolar stars.
Quite an experience you must agree, but it means all you can
do now is shine for 20,000,000 years or so until you become
a Red Giant or White Dwarf or Black Hole, at which point you
can crawl back gratefully to 13.

<102>

Rushing headlong from the sarcophagus, you run full tilt into
Spider Simpson who's admiring a statue of an Apis bull. "No,
no," you cry, "I will not do it!"

"Do what?" asks Spider, who's obviously forgotten all about
the bet.

"I will not hide myself overnight in the sarcophagus of
Nectanebo however many toffee apples you offer me!"
you exclaim.

After which you leave school, find a steady job, get married,
raise 2.4 children, retire to a cottage in the country and
eventually die of old age. Thus completing what must be the
shortest, most boring adventure in the history of game
books. Unless, of course, you want to start again.

103

For a moment everything is confused as you speak the spell aloud, then your mind slowly clears and you find you are no longer in the Pharaoh's palace. Instead, you are standing on a huge square rocky plateau overlooking to the east the palm groves of a broad, slow river you can only imagine must be the Nile.

An instant of panic seizes you. But the panic slowly changes to wonderment as you look around. Between the Nile and the vast wasteland of the Libyan desert to the west rises a series of structures that are truly awesome. Three mountains of stone rise to the sky before you. Even the smallest is monstrous, but the largest is a sight the like of which you have never seen before.

It is a towering pyramid that gleams pure white in the high North African sun, while the cap of pure gold at the pyramid's apex sparkles and shines. You are looking at the Great Pyramid of Egypt, one of the Seven Wonders of the Ancient World. You stand dumbstruck.

Which is a change for you, but not all that useful. If you ever get your act together, you should remember you've got a job to do. So study the map of the Giza complex on page 63 taken from your *Brief History of Ancient Egypt*, and make up your mind where you want to start exploring.

104

Even as you give the answer, you have a horrible suspicion you've chosen wrong. "So," he hisses "you decide to insult me, do you?" With which he returns to his former stony state.

You tense and close your eyes, waiting in terror for the dreadful doom that is about to befall you. There is a ghastly sensation in your stomach, a driving pain in your head, a massive weakness in your limbs, but after a minute you realise all this is just your imagination and absolutely nothing has happened. As a matter of fact, the magic tingling has died down and the paralysis that held you on the slab has disappeared.

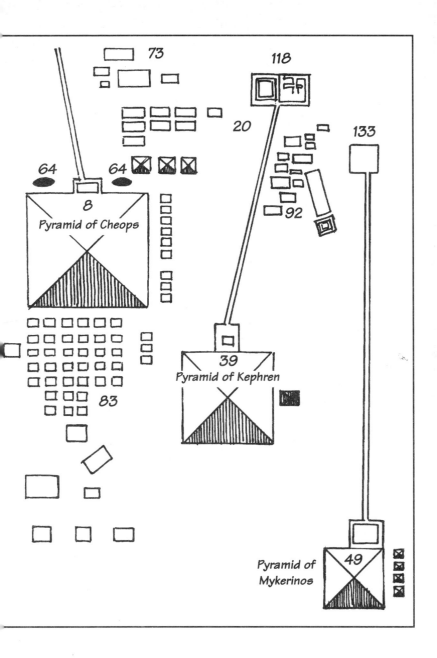

73

118

20

133

64   64

8
Pyramid of Cheops

92

83

39
Pyramid of Kephren

Pyramid of
Mykerinos   49

Your relief is so profound that you race from the chamber as fast as your newly-mobile legs will carry you, stopping only when you have left the Great Pyramid and emerged into the sunshine. You look around to try to find out where you are.

As well you might. Roll one die. Score 1 or 2 and you're at 73. Score 3 or 4 and you're at 92. Score 5 or 6 and you're at 49.

Nothing's happened.

You've pronounced the names, but nothing's happened. You're certainly not dead, but you're still lying in this stupid sarcophagus looking up at the roof of the secret chamber inside the ... wait a minute, it's not the same roof! What's more, there are voices all around you.

You clamber to your feet and start to climb out of the sarcophagus with mounting excitement. You're back in the British Museum! You're definitely back in the British Museum!

A group of Japanese tourists is packed into the Egyptian Gallery, but fortunately they all have their back to you taking photographs of the Sekhmet statue. But Spider Simpson is looking in the right direction and staring at you wide-eyed. "Where on earth have you come from?" he gasps. "When I looked into that sarcophagus a minute ago, it was empty!"

"Actually I've just come from a secret chamber in the inside of the Great Pyramid," you tell him smugly. "You owe me an awful lot of toffee apples."

"Pull the other one," says Spider.

It suddenly occurs to you that your whole experience in Ancient Egypt is pretty unbelievable. In fact, you're beginning to wonder about it yourself. Now you're back, it's certainly taken on a dream-like quality.

So what do you say to Spider? You can be sensible and admit you were dreaming at 93 or stupid and insist you time-travelled at 160.

As the slab withdraws, you realise you are faced with a choice. The passageway you're in continues to descend, but with the slab out of the way you can now see it's joined by a second passageway sloping upwards.

Will you continue downwards with the passage you're in at 7 or take the upward sloping passage at 18?

Seventeen metres further on the passageway ends in a blank wall.

What a bummer! The only thing you can do is retrace your steps. This leaves you free to try jumping into that pit you just passed at 117 or returning all the way up the descending passage to the junction with the ascending passage at 18, or selecting another destination from your map at 103. Unless, of course, you search for a secret door in this apparent dead end at 157.

The procession of priests passes several stone built temples, then turns off to march towards an enormous, brightly-painted building which seems to be made from mud brick. "God's House," murmurs a priest reverentially.

"How come it's made from mud?" you ask.

"What else would we use?" he asks in a superior way.

"Stone," you snap, miffed.

"We only use stone to build our temples," says the priest. "And, of course, our Houses of Eternity."

You wonder what a House of Eternity might be, but before you can ask, a contingent of guards marches forward from the brightly-painted building to meet up with your group.

"Who approaches God's House?" asks the guard captain.

"God's Servants approach God's House," replies one of the priests.

"Then pass, God's Servants," says the guard.

It's obviously a ritual response, but as your group moves forward, the guard glances at you and remarks, "God's been wanting to meet this one – better not keep Him waiting."

This is getting downright weird. You climb into a sarcophagus and next thing you know you're in a place that looks suspiciously like Ancient Egypt, being marched into a glorified mud hut to meet God, who's apparently expecting you. This could be your last chance to escape. Maybe a surprise attack at 122 would do the trick. Otherwise you're about to find out what God looks like at 44.

As your hand touches the precious object, a bolt of lightning strikes down from the cloudless sky, the ground heaves in a violent earthquake and a weird light wraps itself around you.

Wouldn't you know it? This is definitely yet another Egyptian curse. Roll one die. Score 1 or 2 and you find yourself magically transported to 64 (without the ankh). Score 3 or 4 and you find yourself transported to 13 (without the ankh). Score 5 or 6 and you find yourself magically transported to 124.

No sooner have the names passed your lips than your head explodes.

Clean up the mess and go to 13.

Nectanebo puts his arm around your shoulder. "So pleased you've made it this far," he murmurs, "but now I think a little talk in private may be the thing. I expect there are many questions you would like to ask." Since he is not wrong there, you follow him like a lamb from the throne room into a private chamber beyond.

You step through the door to discover there's a lion crouching in the corner.

What is it with this place? Hassles never stop! That lion's not about to hang about, so you'd better decide what to do about it. Frankly you've only really got two choices. You can hurl yourself upon the beast at 156, or you can leave Nectanebo to deal with it at 140.

As you move towards the steps you notice to your relief that there's a little oil lamp beside the first one. You pick it up, expecting it to be empty, but to your surprise it contains a small quantity of sesame oil which burns with a bright but smokeless flame. Holding the lamp aloft, you begin to make your way down the steps.

As you do so, the slab closes behind you of its own accord. In sudden panic, you turn back and try to move the stone. It will not budge. There is no way back. The only thing you can do is follow the stairs downwards and hope to find another exit.

So you follow them downwards, growing more and more nervous of the darkness beyond the flickering lamplight, until you reach a subterranean chamber with a single exit corridor. In the centre of the floor is an open sarcophagus. Inside it is an intact mummy case.

Do you examine that sarcophagus more closely at 100, or make for that exit corridor at 79 as fast as your legs will carry you?

Feeling a bit of a prat, you pronounce the Pharaoh's name aloud. The sound reverberates in the enclosed space and at once you experience the unmistakable tingle that tells you there's magic about.

You look expectantly at the slab. There is a low grinding noise like the sound of stone on stone.

At which the great slab retracts, leaving you free to proceed to 89.

"I'll have this one," you tell her, indicating the scarab. "What does it do?"

"Not a lot, I'm afraid," Isis tells you. "But it really does look very pretty."

With which she banishes you to 103 to seek another destination.

The only light in this building is the sunlight filtering through the open door: there are no windows at all. But while it's gloomy by contrast with the courtyard outside, you can still plainly see a forest of enormous pillars, each one brightly painted with Egyptian scenes.

You wander around for a while, wondering how on earth a place like this could have been built before heavy cranes and bulldozers were invented.

Then you find another open doorway into a second chamber. As you step inside, you realise this one is seriously gloomy. It takes a moment for your eyes to adjust before you can see inside.

Not that there's much to see. At the far end of the chamber there's something that looks like a very large stone sentry box with double doors tied shut with string.

And that's about all.

If you can bear to stick around this creepy inner chamber, you can look inside the stone sentry box at 32. But you might be better off returning to the outer courtyard at 152 to see if anything's happened there.

You throw yourself to one side as the scorpion moves to attack and the poisoned sting whistles past your ear. This thing is so fast, it will be a miracle if you get in the first blow in the combat to come.

But let's hope you do, because if that scorpion manages even one successful hit against you, you're dead from poisoning. As against that, if you manage even one successful hit against it with Osiris' flail, it's dead from magic, since the flail will kill an opponent with a single blow. Throw a single die to find out how many times you can use the flail in this way. If the scorpion kills you, the burning pain will stop at 13. If you kill the scorpion, take the exit door to your right and turn to 45.

The rubble gives way beneath your feet. As you pick yourself up, your attention is caught by the corner of an ancient casket half buried in the debris. You pick it up, dust it off and are about to open it when you notice a one-word hieroglyphic inscription on the lid:

If you want to open the casket, you can do so at 153. If not, you can leave it where you found it and try climbing out of the pit at 127.

You are surrounded by the monolithic stone block walls of an ancient temple. A strong wind causes sand to sting your eyes. Uncertain of what you are looking for, you begin to explore.

"Pharaoh Khefra's Valley Temple," mutters a voice on your left. You glance over to find a little weather-beaten man, whose face looks vaguely familiar, squatting at the base of a broken pillar.

"Pardon?"

"This used to be King Khefra's temple," the little man repeats. "In the old days. Bit broken up now. Linked to his pyramid by a causeway – you probably noticed," calls the little man. "Used to have some remarkable statues of the king. Carved from diorite, about the hardest stone you can find. Had to go all the way to Nubia to get it. Of course most of the statues have been nicked by now. Can't keep anything to yourself these days."

You nod politely and start to move off.

"How about a little present?" calls the little man.

You stop again. "Why should I give you a little present?"

"Because I gave you the information about the temple."

You frown. "But I didn't ask you for the information."

The little man stands up and brushes some sand off your shoulder. "How about giving me something for that?"

"I didn't ask you to brush me

down either."

"You look neater now," he says.

You're close to shouting. "I don't care if I look neater – I'm not giving you a present!"

"How about buying something then?" says the little man. "I do a nice line in statues." He reaches into the linen bag on the ground beside him and takes out several ugly little figurines of Egyptian gods so badly made you could scarcely tell the difference between Isis and Anubis.

"I don't want any," you say.

"How about a nice talisman then?" He shakes the bag out onto the floor. Several more items of tat roll towards your feet. "See the way they went towards you?" he says excitedly. "That's an omen. Means you were meant to buy one. Look at the quality."

You look at the quality, which is dreadful. But the little man rushes over exclaiming, "Feel how much magic is in them!" One by one he presses three small talismans into your hand.

The first looks for all the world like a dung beetle. The second is an eye that seems to be suffering from a hangover. The third is a little matchstick man with no legs. There is not the slightest hint of magical power in any of them.

This clown is going to persecute you until you buy something or run. If you want to run, head for 103 where you can select another destination. If you prefer to buy him off, negotiate for the dung beetle at 2, the eye at 16 or the man at 30.

<119>

You find yourself standing at the mouth of a horizontal passageway. Behind you is a descending passage. Almost at your feet is a narrow shaft that plunges straight down towards the bedrock below the massive pyramid.

If you want to try negotiating that shaft, you can do so at 76. The horizontal passage looks a lot easier at 129. Or you can take the descending passage which will eventually get you

out of the pyramid altogether so you can return to your map at 103 and select another destination.

With a gigantic crash the entire pyramid falls on your head.

Dig yourself out at 13.

No sooner have the names passed your lips than your head explodes.

Clean up the mess and go to 13.

There are easily two dozen guards, all heavily armed, plus half as many priests, at least some of whom appear to be carrying daggers. You hurl yourself at the guard captain, figuring that if you can get him out of the way quickly, you should be able to make your escape in the ensuing confusion.

We'll see. The guard captain is actually recovering from a recent run-in with the Persians, so he has only 30 Life Points – and you certainly get in first strike due to that famous element of surprise. As against that, if you don't finish him off in three combat rounds, his companions will come to the rescue and drag you off screaming to 44. If, that is, he hasn't managed to kill you in self-defence, in which case you can carry yourself off screaming to 13. But if your lunatic plan succeeds, you can in fact make your escape to 17.

Even as you give the answer, you have a horrible suspicion you've chosen wrong. "So," he hisses "you decide to insult me, do you?" With which he twitches an eyebrow and returns to his former stony state.

You tense and close your eyes, waiting in terror for the dreadful doom that is about to befall you. There is a ghastly sensation in your stomach, a driving pain in your head, a massive weakness

n your limbs, but after a minute you realise all this is just your
imagination and absolutely nothing has happened. As a matter of
fact, the magic tingling has died down and the paralysis that held
you on the slab has disappeared.

Your relief is so profound that you race from the chamber as fast
as your newly-mobile legs will carry you, stopping only when
you have left the Great Pyramid and emerged into the sunshine.
When your panic subsides, you look around to try to find out
where you are.

*As well you might. Roll one die. Score 1 or 2 and you're at 73;
score 3 or 4 and you're at 92; score 5 or 6 and you're at 49.*

‹124›

There's desert all around you as far as the eye can see. Scorpions
play around your feet and vultures circle overhead. In your hand
is clutched an electrum ankh.

*For whatever good that will do you in finding your way back to
civilization. Throw one die. Score 1 and the scorpions get you
and you go to 13. Score 2 and the vultures get you and you go
to 13. Score anything else and you'll stagger into 103 very
dehydrated, extremely hungry, and with half your Life Points
missing, but at least capable of selecting another destination
from your map.*

‹125›

The papyrus fragments are in no particular order and seem to be
all that's left of a very much longer work. From various clues,
you deduce that Herodotus was a Greek author who lived about a
hundred years before the time you're in now. Although his
History is supposed to be about the Greco-Persian Wars, the bits
you've found all seem to be about Egypt and its distant past:

*Legend tells of a secret temple hidden beneath the sphinx,
but the priests of yore protected it with many spells and
traps. Do not enter it without the Eye of Horus for
protection ...*

There is, if ancient records are to be believed, a magical sarcophagus within a chamber of the Great Pyramid which activates only when the name of Pharaoh Cheops has been pronounced, along with the name of the god who carries crook and flail ...

Now turn back to the section you just left and get on with your adventure.

<126>

As your finger touches the slab, the stone dissolves into dust, and you enter another low-ceilinged passageway leading into a well-proportioned chamber. The walls, floor and ceiling are all constructed of finely polished red granite blocks.

You stare open-mouthed at ornaments of gold, heaps of gemstones, caskets of pearls, artefacts of silver and electrum, priceless scrolls, and wonderful substances such as malleable glass. In the exact centre of the room sits a large, lidless, sarcophagus of chocolate-coloured granite. In this reclines a mummy with a massive ruby set in the middle of its forehead.

You have found the treasure trove!

For a moment you stand joyfully just looking at the hoard. Then, as you promised the Pharaoh, you scribble down directions to this secret chamber and attach the scrap of papyrus to the pigeon he gave you. You release the bird, wholly confident it will find its exit from the pyramid and carry the message to Nectanebo.

But now, duty done, you must find the gateway back to your own time. You look around the chamber. Climbing into one sarcophagus brought you here to Egypt: logic dictates that climbing into another might get you home again. You move towards the sarcophagus. As you do so, the mummy sits up and turns towards you.

If you're going to climb into that sarcophagus it will be over this thing's dead body. The mummy has 60 Life Points (in a manner of speaking) but that's not the bad news. The bad news is that the ruby in its forehead focuses psychic energy like a laser, enabling the brute to zap you with a mental blast which will remove a cool 20 Life Points from you every time the mummy scores a hit. If, as seems likely, you lose this grossly uneven contest, you can knit your brain back together again at 13. If you win, you can tackle the problem of getting home again at 9.

127

The walls are rough and it certainly isn't far from the top, but as you start to climb you realise getting out isn't going to be a piece of cake, since every hand or foothold you reach for seems to crumble at your touch.

Better throw one die. Score 1, 2, 3 or 4 and you climb safely out and can head for the exit passage at 107, or even retrace your steps along the descending passage to the junction with the ascending passage at 18, not to mention leaving the pyramid altogether to select another destination from 103. Score 5 or 6 and escape proves impossible so you slowly starve to death at 13.

128

Moving quickly, you hoist yourself up and half fall over the lip of Nectanebo's sarcophagus. There's no lid, so you tumble (painfully) all the way in. The sarcophagus is so deep you're completely hidden, unless some-one takes the trouble of climbing up to look over the top.

You lie down on your back and fold your arms across your chest. You can see the British Museum ceiling. It's very boring. After a while your eyes begin to droop, despite the noise of visitors, and you feel yourself drifting towards sleep. Then, suddenly, you are aware of a young face staring down at you in complete amazement. "Dad!" yells the child. "There's a mummy in here!"

Your eyes open fully with a start and you make to sit up. "It's alive!" the child screams. "It's coming to get me!"

"Come down from there you little brat," a male voice growls.

The child's face disappears abruptly and shortly afterwards you hear the bell that warns visitors the museum is closing. Within fifteen minutes, the whole place is silent as the tomb. You make yourself comfortable – or as comfortable as you can in a granite sarcophagus. In a moment you are snoring gently and dreaming of a toffee apple the size of Cleopatra's Needle. You look forward to seeing Spider Simpson's face tomorrow.

Maybe. Roll one die. Score 1, 2 or 3 and go to 86. Score 4, 5 or 6 and go to 144. Anything else takes you to 13 (just joking).

The passageway has such a low ceiling that you're forced to stoop a little to make your way along it. But there are no blockages, so you eventually find your way to a near-square limestone chamber with a rough floor and gabled limestone ceiling. A niche in the eastern wall contains a larger-than-life-size statue of an ibis-headed Egyptian god.

Since the statue is the only thing in the room, you walk across to take a closer look. As you do so, you suddenly notice that inset into the rough floor directly in front of this statue is a smooth granite slab.

The question is, are you so interested in the statue that you're prepared to take the risk of stepping onto that granite slab? If you want to risk it, you can do so at 158. If not, you can go back the way you came to 119.

Cautiously you call on the deity to open the sarcophagus. Your voice echoes eerily in the confines of this gloomy chamber, but nothing happens. You call again, a little nervously. Still nothing happens. You call a third time ...

There is a thunderclap so loud and immediate that you come close to jumping out of your skin. The chamber fills with smoke and flashing lights, and you find yourself faced with the towering figure of the god Osiris, looking much like his statues, wearing bandages and carrying his famous crook and flail.

He fixes you with a gimlet eye. "You don't seriously think I'm the deity of war, do you?" he asks. "My bag is actually fertility, although I often double up as king of the dead. In fact, I think I feel quite insulted by your invocation."

With which he twitches his little finger, magically transporting you out of the pyramid at a loss of 10 Life Points. If this kills you, go to 13. If it doesn't, you'll find that you're now at 103 where you can select your next destination.

"As a matter of fact, I *do* have a purple scarab," you tell the little man. "Straight swap?"

He nods, but then, as he pockets your scarab he suggests, "Want to toss for them, double or quits?"

"You mean if I win the toss, I get my ankh and scarab back and if you win, you get your Bastet statues back?" you ask.

"Exactly!" says the little man.

"How can we toss when coins haven't been invented yet?"

"Nectanebo's issued the first Egyptian coin early this morning," says the little man promptly, "and I just happen to have one with me."

If you want to risk double or quits, turn to 151. Otherwise turn to 103 and select another destination.

Roll one die.

Score 1 or 2 and your Life Points return instantly to their maximum if they were below maximum when you rubbed the ring. (Nothing happens if they weren't.)

Score 3 or 4 and any one opponent turns into a scarab beetle if you rubbed the ring while you were in a fight. (Nothing happens if you weren't.)

Score 5 or 6 and you automatically succeed in your Absolutely Anything Roll if you were attempting an Absolutely Anything Roll when you rubbed the ring. (Nothing happens if you weren't.)

Hope this helps. Now get back to the section you were in when you rubbed the magic ring.

133

This is yet another Egyptian temple, and while it has mostly fallen to ruins, it seems as if a full-scale restoration programme is in progress. Large numbers of workmen are demolishing the more dangerous structures and carefully rebuilding, often with the original stone.

A little distance from the temple itself, a group of men is quarrying a massive granite block. One man, using a simple pick of hardened copper, has cut a long channel the width of one leg, to separate the block from the bedrock. As he works, two others are dressing the exposed surface of the block by tapping it with rounded stones, each one roughly the size of a small melon.

When the channel is finished, wedges driven into small holes along the length of the block cause it to split cleanly away. Although this single block must weigh at least four tonnes, it is transported easily to the temple site by dragging it along a set of polished wooden rails, lubricated by a little water.

In the temple itself, mud ramps have been constructed to give access to the higher reaches of the walls. You watch as the great block is dragged up one of them, then manoeuvred into place by means of long wooden levers.

But fascinating though the process is to watch, you have more urgent things to do. You begin to search the ruins for some clue to the treasure the Pharaoh is seeking. You are about to give up when you hear an excited shout from a workman. You run across to find him holding a dusty, cracked diorite stone slab with a faded inscription cut into its surface. "What is it?" you ask.

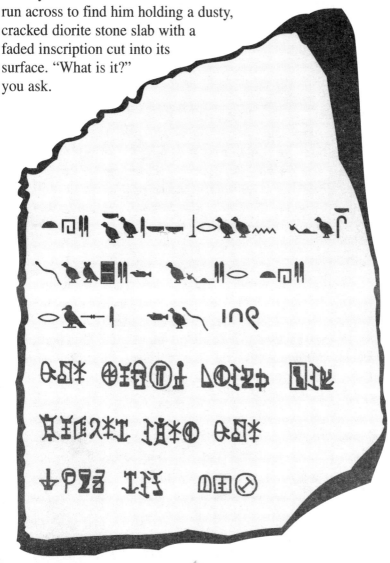

The workman shrugs. "Thought it might be a treasure map when I found it, but the inscription's just a load of rubbish about wildlife – at least the hieroglyphics are: I can't make head nor tail of the other stuff." He hands the slab across. "Here, you have it if you want."

"Thanks," you say uncertainly. Although you can't make head nor tail of the second inscription either – the markings don't look at all like hieroglyphs – there's something about the slab that looks vaguely familiar. On impulse you take out your copy of the *Brief History of Ancient Egypt*. Your instinct was correct. The slab in your hand looks a little like the famous Rosetta Stone which was used to crack the mystery of the hieroglyphs.

Probably best to hold onto it, since you never know when something like this could come in handy. You might even try translating the hieroglyphs some time when you've nothing better to do. In the meantime, since there doesn't seem to be much else for you in this area, it's time you headed back to 103 to pick another destination.

Even as you give the answer, you have a horrible suspicion you've chosen wrong. "So," he hisses "you have studied the gods of Egypt, have you? Take that!" With which he twitches his little finger. At once the chamber is filled with magical blue light. For a moment your whole body feels as if it has been stuffed with sherbet fizz, while your mind whirls off beyond the furthest reaches of the galaxy.

When it returns, you discover to your delight that not only have you been cured of every wound you ever sustained, but your maximum Life Points has actually been increased by ten.

"Now be off with you," grins Thoth. At once the paralysis in your body breaks and you scurry from the chamber before this animated statue changes its mind.

And don't even think of stopping scurrying until you reach 71.

135

"Think you can threaten me?" you growl back. "I'll have you know I eat louts like you for breakfast." With which pleasantry you hurl yourself upon him.

This may be a good time to mention Eye-Gor has 60 Life Points and that mallet of his does +5 damage. If you manage to dispatch him, you can get back to your deal about the tablet at 58. If you don't, you get to keep your statue of Bastet for company at 13.

136

You find yourself marching with considerable trepidation between two ranks of hairless priests. Close up, you can see that they've not simply shaved their heads and faces, but their arms, legs and, presumably, every other part of their body as well. They also look – and smell – remarkably clean.

You emerge onto an avenue lined on both sides with sphinxes headed with rams. These gaze down from their pedestals at you with blank stone eyes.

"Where are we going?" you ask the priest nearest you, realising as you do so that you're speaking the same archaic tongue as he does.

"You're going to see God," he growls.

Oh, wow, are they going to kill you this early in the adventure? But what else could 'going to see God' mean? You may want to make a break for it – if so, you'll have to risk an Absolutely Anything Roll. If it succeeds, you escape to 17. If it fails, you continue to be escorted all the way to 108. If it kills you, then you're hacked to pieces at 13. Of course, you don't have to attempt an escape at all, in which case you will be taken to see God at 108.

137

No sooner have the names passed your lips than your head explodes.

Clean up the mess and go to 13.

138

You push the door and step into a cramped stone chamber beyond. You freeze as a scorpion the size of a small dog rises up directly in front of you, its tail drawn back ready to sting. It is clear that even a single strike against you will kill outright.

But what to do? If you turn back now, you're likely to be trapped in that maze of passageways, although you can risk this at 29. Your other option is to fight the scorpion at 116.

139

"I'll have this one," you tell her, indicating the orb. "What does it do?"

"It will completely paralyse as many enemies as a single die roll indicates," Isis tells you, "You can use it three times before it shatters."

With which she banishes you to 103 to seek another destination.

140

Nectanebo walks over and tickles the lion behind his ears. The creature purrs like a cat and rubs against the Pharaoh's leg.

"His name's Archimedes," he says. "After that Sicilian mathematician who's due to be born in a few years – around 298 B.C., I believe. But I'm sure you don't want to talk about that. I expect you have one or two questions you'd like to ask me."

You settle for the question that's most important to you. "What am I doing here?"

"Good question," says the Pharaoh. Then, instead of answering it, he continues along his own train of thought.

"The important thing you need to know is what old Wallis Budge said about me, you know, the former Keeper of Egyptian Antiquities in the British Museum. Before your time, of course.

" 'But of all the Egyptians who were skilled in working magic, Nectanebo, the last native king of Egypt, about 358 B.C., was the chief, if we may believe the Greek tradition ... '

"From a book he's going to write called *Egyptian Magic*."

"You're a magician?" you ask sceptically.

"That's how I know about the future. That's how I brought you back in time to Ancient Egypt. You're wearing a different body, of course, but you've probably noticed that already."

You hadn't, but now you think about it, you realise your legs are a bit longer, your skin is a little darker and your eyes have an Oriental fold at each side. No wonder you're able to speak the language. At the same time, you note you're still wearing your old clothes, which explains why so many people here have looked at you oddly. There's even your copy of *A Brief History of Ancient Egypt* in the pocket of your shirt.

"Where's my old body?" you ask.

"Still quite safe lying in my sarcophagus in the British Museum," says Nectanebo. "It isn't a sarcophagus, of course. It's a time machine disguised as one. I made it as a sort of net to catch somebody from year 2000. You're a little bit early, but no harm in that."

"But why do you want somebody from the year 2000?" you ask, now thoroughly confused.

"To help me defeat the Persians, of course." Nectanebo looks you straight in the eye. "Will you help?"

Oh wow! From everything you've heard, those Persians were tough fighters. If you think one young person can make a real difference in the Ancient World, listen to what Nectanebo has to say at 15. If not, you can always decline politely at 3.

Cautiously you call on the deity to open the sarcophagus. Your voice echoes eerily in the confines of this gloomy chamber, but nothing happens. You call again, a little nervously. Still nothing happens. You call a third time ...

There is a thunderclap so loud and immediate that you come close to jumping out of your skin. The chamber fills with billowing smoke and flashing lights and you find yourself faced with the towering figure of the goddess Isis, wearing a very flattering figure-hugging translucent gown and a head-dress representing the crescent moon.

She glares at you. "I can't imagine where you got the idea I was the deity of war. I am, I'll have you know, mother of Horus, wife of Osiris and protector of the dead. I'm also known for my magical abilities, as you're about to find out."

With which she twitches her little finger, magically transporting you out of the pyramid at a loss of 10 Life Points. If this kills you, go to 13. If it doesn't, you'll find when your head clears that you're now at 103 where you can select your next destination.

Somehow you feel better with some idea where to dig. Not that it makes any practical difference. You're still up to your eyebrows in sand, the hot sun still beams down on your head, the huge statue still looms over you and the hole you're making just gets bigger ... and bigger ... and bigger ...

Wait a minute, you've hit on something! You truly, really have! There's a stone slab down here with an indentation the size and shape of a human hand. And when you slide your own hand into it, the slab lifts up as smooth as butter. You stare at a flight of stone steps descending into darkness.

Do you want to descend the steps? If so, turn to 112. If not, you can choose another destination at 103.

No sooner have the names passed your lips than your head explodes.

Clean up the mess and go to 13.

Your eyes open abruptly of their own accord. It's still dark, but you've obviously slept soundly right through most of the night, so dawn should be breaking very soon.

A bubble of delight pops pleasantly inside your head. Boy, will Spider Simpson be annoyed! Boy, will he be mortified when he has to buy you toffee apples every week! Now all you have to do is climb out of the sarcophagus and wait until the Museum opens, then mingle with the early morning crowds and slip out into the old familiar London rain.

As your eyes adjust, you realise it is not entirely dark. Somewhere beyond the sarcophagus, the Museum authorities must have left a small night light glowing. The sarcophagus feels more cramped somehow, although that's probably just because you've grown a bit stiff while sleeping. Although it seems far more shallow as well and it's difficult to see what that has to do with stiffness. At the same time it feels more comfortable, as if you were lying on something soft. It's certainly easier to climb out than it was to climb in ...

You're not in the British Museum!

You stand frozen with shock. The towering stela of Nectanebo has disappeared. So have various other exhibits. But worse than that, the very building you were in has changed. In fact it doesn't look like a building of any sort. If anything, it feels as if you're standing in an enormous rock-hewn cavern.

Your paralysis breaks and you look around. This is creepy. You're definitely in a cavern of some sort, but it looks as if it's man-made, hacked from the solid rock. And it's far from empty.

The light is actually coming from some oil lamps which illuminate a veritable treasure-trove. Huge though the cavern is, it is jam-packed with various goods – statues, beds, chairs, chests, caskets, vases, even chariots, model boats, and something that looks like a bird's perch covered in gold leaf.

You turn and look behind you, then promptly wish you hadn't.

Instead of the deep, empty sarcophagus of Nectanebo you climbed into, you see you've climbed out of a smaller sarcophagus with a mummy already inside it. You start to gag. You've been sleeping on top of a rotting mummy!

Hurriedly you look away. Your heart thumps furiously as you look for a way out. The cavern itself is so enormous it's difficult to see beyond the circle of dim lamplight, but you seem to make out the entrance to a passage running upwards, and what looks like an open ante-chamber running off the main cavern.

Which means you've three options. You can explore the passage at 24. You can explore the ante-chamber at 48. Or, as a fairly gross long shot, you can climb into the sarcophagus with the rotting mummy at 63 and see if that sends you safely back to the British Museum.

Nope, no secret entrance here.

You can examine the south face at 65, the east face at 74 or the north face at 37. Or, if you get bored with the whole thing, you can always go back to 103 and select another destination from your map.

"As a matter of fact, I do have an electrum ankh," you tell the little man. "Straight swap?"

"Suits me," he nods, taking a small cat-like sandstone statue from his pack and handing it across to you. As he pockets your electrum ankh, he adds, "Want another one? You can have it for a purple scarab. Not interested in any other colour, mind you."

Why you'd want two statues of Bastet is beyond me, but if you do and happen to have a purple scarab about your person, you can acquire the second one at 131. Otherwise, you can return to your map at 103 and select another destination.

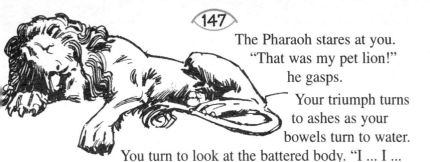

The Pharaoh stares at you. "That was my pet lion!" he gasps.

Your triumph turns to ashes as your bowels turn to water. You turn to look at the battered body. "I ... I ... I'm sorry," you stammer. "I had no idea – "

"Don't you read history?" shouts Nectanebo. "Don't you know nearly every Egyptian Pharaoh kept a pet lion? It's a status symbol!" He swallows hard to get his temper under control. "Well, I can get him back on his feet again, but only if somebody – " he glares at you "donates 25 Life Points."

But can you afford them? If the loss of a further 25 Life Points kills you, join poor old Leo in 13. If you manage, you can breathe a sigh of relief and turn to 140.

"I just happen to have a small statue of Bastet about my person," you tell the foreman. "And I would certainly be interested in exchanging it for your ancient tablet."

"Fine by me," says the foreman.

But as he reaches into his tool-kit for the tablet, a rough-looking workman with an enormous mallet appears beside him. "Here, Khonsu, I told you I wanted that tablet. The kid gets it over my dead body!"

The foreman Khonsu looks at you helplessly. "I'm afraid if you really want it, you're going to have to fight Eye-Gor for it."

"Yus," growls Eye-Gor, waving his mallet threateningly.

Well, you don't have to fight this lout if you don't want to. You can always forego the tablet and return to your map at 103 to select another destination. But if you're feeling lucky, you can always make his day at 135.

You pick up the best of the guards' +10 swords and stick it in your belt in case it might come in handy at a later time. You're about to walk away when you notice both guards are wearing curious charms around their necks. The charms look like this:

While a good many Egyptians wear charms of one sort or another, these items look far too valuable for lowly soldiers. You take one off and examine it closely. Unless you're very much mistaken, it's gold inlaid with lapis lazuli and diamonds, a trinket that must be worth a king's ransom – and here are two of them within your grasp! On impulse you hang the charm you've been examining around your neck.

At once a voice whispers in your ear, "You are growing sleepy ... your eyelids are heavy... your body is relaxing ... you will listen and obey as you fall deeper and deeper asleep ... deeper and deeper asleep ... deeper and deeper asleep ... "

This is incredible! You're actually being hypnotised long distance by somebody using the charm as a mystic link! Instantly you apply your massive willpower to fighting off the influence.

And fail. In thirty seconds you are walking like a zombie towards 44.

"What's the little service?" you ask suspiciously. You are sure it is a translation of some obscure message from the hieroglyphic. All through this rotten adventure you seem to be translating.

"You have to agree to do it before I tell you," the little man says slyly.

"All right! All right! I agree!" How bad can another boring translation job be?

The little man nods at someone behind you. "I want you to beat him up," he says. "He insulted the quality of my goods."

You turn to discover standing behind you the biggest, meanest, toughest Egyptian you have ever seen. He's over six foot tall and has the sort of build that makes the Muscles from Brussels look like the Limp Leek from Leeds.

"Nothing personal, but I've given my word," you say as you bop him on the nose.

In this punch-up no weapons are allowed – it's fists only. You punch at dice damage only, but Mr Universe hits with a massive +8 due to his muscles.

When either of you drops below 10 Life Points, the fight stops and the one with most Life Points at that time is declared the winner. If your opponent accidentally kills you, go to 13.

If he brings you below 10 Life Points without killing you, pick yourself up and skulk off to 103 without the item the little man was trying to sell you. If you bring him below 10 Life Points, thus winning the fight, take the talisman you chose to buy and stride off to 103.

151

"Okay," you say, "I'll toss you."

Although what you actually *do* is roll a die. Score 1, 2 or 3 and you lose your two statues of Bastet to the little man. Score 4, 5 or 6 and you win back your electrum ankh and purple scarab. If you're happy with the result, turn to 103 and select another destination from your map. If not, you can always try taking your property back by force at 22.

152

It's a relief to step back out into the sunshine, but your relief is very short-lived when you discover the courtyard is now packed full of completely hairless men. One of them spots you immediately. "There's a stranger in the temple!" he shouts in an archaic language that, somehow, you understand perfectly.

Scores of eyes swing in your direction. "Seize him!" another shouts. In seconds you're surrounded by hairless men smelling of the sort of incense and oil that marks them at once as priests.

No way you can fight this many. Go with them to 136.

No way you can fight this many. Go with them to 136.

153

Bravely you flick open the casket. At once a deep voice echoes through the chamber: "You have been smitten by the curse of +2!"

Inside the casket is a ceramic jar of healing salve which will restore you to full Life Points every time you apply it to the pulses on your wrists.

Nice find. Throw one die and add two to your score to find out how many applications are left in the jar. This must be the dumbest curse the Ancient Egyptians ever placed. Fancy having to add two to every die score you make from now on. Now all you have to do is climb out of the pit at 127 and be on your way.

154

Cautiously you call on the deity to open the sarcophagus. Your voice echoes eerily in the confines of this gloomy chamber, but nothing happens. You call again, a little nervously. Still nothing happens. You call a third time ...

There is a thunderclap so loud and immediate that you come close to jumping out of your skin. The chamber fills with billowing smoke and flashing lights and you find yourself faced with the towering figure of the goddess Sekhmet, a woman who somehow seems to have grown the head of a lion.
"What can I do for you?" she growls.

You swallow nervously. "You wouldn't take the lid off this sarcophagus, would you?" She throws a disgusted glance towards heaven, growls again, then disappears.

"Hey, wait a minute!" you call. "I'm sure I read somewhere that you were the deity of war. I mean, you can't just – "

You stop, embarrassed, as you notice the lid of the sarcophagus is now lying on the floor. Excitedly you run across and look in. To your intense disappointment, the sarcophagus is empty. No treasure, no wondrous artefacts, not even a rotting mummy.

You're about to turn away when you notice a scrap of papyrus tucked into one corner. Leaning forward perilously, you fish it out and unfold it.

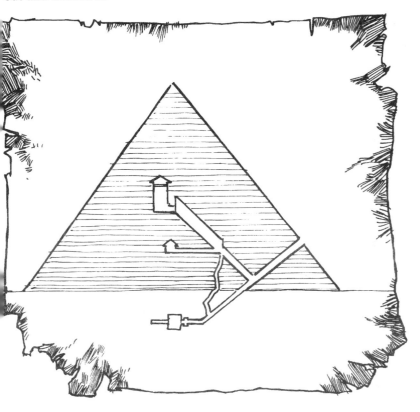

It seems to be a map of the interior of a pyramid. There's no indication of which one, but it doesn't seem to be the one you're in at the moment.

Speaking of which, since there doesn't seem to be much more for you here, take the exit passageway to 61.

With a sigh of relief you examine the tablet. It certainly looks peculiar, and the hieroglyphs are so small and faded you might have a problem translating them.

Difficult to say whether this was worth the trouble, although it might come in handy later. Meanwhile, you'd better get back to your map at 103 and select another destination.

156

"Stand back!" you cry heroically. You beat your chest, yodel like Tarzan and hurl yourself upon the beast.

Which has 120 Life Points and +10 fang and claw damage. If this lion eats you, it will spit your bits back to 13. If you slay the lion, you may be in more trouble than you imagine at 147.

157

Nope, not a sign of a door here.

Double bummer! The only thing you can do is retrace your steps. This leaves you free to try jumping into that pit you just passed at 117, or returning to the descending passage to the junction with the ascending passage at 18, or leaving the pyramid altogether so you can select another destination from your map at 103.

You step onto the slab. There is a loud ringing noise and the familiar tingle of Ancient Egyptian magic. A creeping paralysis seizes your limbs. The closed eyes of the god flick open.

"I am Thoth, god of magic, reckoning, learning, writing and ... If you can tell me what else I am god of, I shall release you. If not, you shall die. So, am I also god of the star Sirius, the constellation Orion, or Earth's satellite the Moon?"

For Sirius, turn to 104; Orion, to 123; the Moon, to 134.

No sooner have the names passed your lips than your head explodes.

Clean up the mess and go to 13.

"Don't think I'll swallow that!" says Spider, turning away. You, too, begin to leave the Egyptian Gallery. Maybe it was all a dream! What a bummer this has all turned out to be!

But as you pass the sarcophagus of Nectanebo, a line of hieroglyphs catches your eye. They look fresher than the rest…

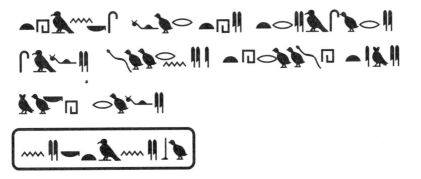

You translate them swiftly, straighten your shoulders, and walk from the Museum with a smug smile on your face.

GAME PLAY SYSTEM
Here's what you'll need to survive this book:

Life Points

Roll one of your dice and multiply the result by ten to give you a Life Point figure between 10 and 60. You're allowed to do this three times and pick the best score out of the three.

Fights

First attack: In any combat situation, begin by rolling one of your dice. Score 4, 5 or 6 and the first attack is yours. Score 1, 2 or 3 and your opponent gets to go first.

Striking blows: Roll both dice to strike a blow or use a weapon. Score 2, 3 or 4 and it counts as a miss. Anything else is a hit and the score comes off your opponent's Life Points. Throw the dice for your opponent in exactly the same way. Any hits scored by him come off your Life Points.

Weapons: If you (or your opponent) are using a weapon, it adds extra damage to a successful hit. The amount of extra damage is given with the weapon. For example, if you find a +5 pistol, it means each time you successfully shoot somebody with it, you add 5 to the damage shown by the dice.

Ammunition: Firearms are useless without ammo. You'll be told when you find a weapon how much ammo it contains. Once out of ammo, you score no extra damage when using a firearm.

Healing

Medicine: Medicine restores Life Points. You'll be told how to calculate the number of restored Points with each medical pack.

Rest: If you can't find medicine when you need it, you can always take a chance on resting. You can rest any time and as often as you like. To do so, throw one of your dice. Score 5 or 6 and you can add that number to your Life Points. Score 3 or 4 and you deduct that number, because you were attacked in your sleep. Score 1 or 2 and you rested without being attacked, but were too nervous to restore any Life Points.

Death

When your Life Points come down to zero, you're dead and you have to start the adventure again from the beginning. When any opponent's Life Points reach zero, they too are dead.

Money

Keep a careful note of any money you may earn or find during your adventure. It could be useful for buying things or (occasionally) bribery.

Experience

Every time you win a fight (and in a few other special circumstances as well) you earn one Experience Point. Keep careful note of the total: 10 Experience Points gives you a Special Life Point. Special Life Points are added to your total just like ordinary Life Points and are lost in fights just like ordinary Life Points. However, if you're killed during an adventure, you can add all your Special Life Points to your score when you're rolling up your Life Points for the next try.

You can add Special Life Points even if you score the absolute maximum of 60 when you're rolling your Life Points. So if you have earned 6 Special Life Points and score 60 on your Life Point roll, your final Life Points will be 66.

Special Life Points carry over to other books in this series.

Absolutely Anything Roll

From time to time during your adventure, you might want to try to do something weird or spectacular. To find out the result, use the Absolutely Anything Roll. Throw both dice.

- Score 2 and you failed to do what you tried to do and killed yourself in the attempt.

- Score 3, 4 or 5 and you failed to do what you tried to do and can't try again.

- Score 6, 7, 8 or 9 and you failed to do what you tried to do but can try just one more time.

- Score 10, 11 or 12 and you succeed.

GLOSSARY

Amulet
A small charm used to ward off evil spirits.

Antimony
A bluish-white element of metallic appearance.

Caliph
The spiritual leader of Islam.

Diorite
A volcanic rock containing quartz.

Electrum
An alloy of silver and gold used in ancient times.

Flail
An implement used for threshing corn.

Gods
The gods of the Ancient Egyptians were the elements around them, such as the Sun or rain. Gradually, however, the Egyptians came to think of their gods as having human qualities. They began to represent them in human form, but with animal heads.

Herodotus
Greek historian alive around 450 B.C.

Hieroglyphs
Characters used in Ancient Egyptian picture writing.

Horus
The heavenly falcon god.

Ka
A person's double who stayed with him or her after death. Food or drink placed in the tomb were meant as offerings to the Ka.

Lapis
A type of stone.

Mastabas
Tombs of Ancient Egyptian nobles.

Papyrus
A reed used for making paper.

Runes
Mystic symbols.

Sarcophagus
A stone coffin.

Sphinx
A monster carved from stone, usually with the head of a man or woman and the body of a lion.

Stela
An upright stone slab.